RHYTHM RIDE

RHYTHM RIDE

A ROAD TRIP THROUGH THE MOTOWN SOUND

ANDREA DAVIS PINKNEY

ROARING BROOK PRESS NEW YORK

Copyright © 2015 by Andrea Davis Pinkney
Published by Roaring Brook Press
Roaring Brook Press is a division of Holtzbrinck Publishing Holdings Limited
Partnership
175 Fifth Avenue, New York, New York 10010
mackids.com

Library of Congress Cataloging-in-Publication Data

Pinkney, Andrea Davis, author.
 Rhythm ride : a road trip through the Motown sound / Andrea Davis Pinkney. —
1st edition.
  pages cm
 Summary: "A narrative history of the Motown music label covering the historical
context, personalities, and ongoing legacy of the "sound of young America." —
Provided by publisher.
 ISBN 978-1-59643-973-3 (hardback) — ISBN 978-1-59643-974-0 (e-book)
 1. Motown Record Corporation—Juvenile literature. 2. Sound recording
industry—United States—Juvenile literature. I. Title.
 ML3792.M67P32 2015
 781.64409774'34—dc23
                                                                    2014045894

Roaring Brook Press books may be purchased for business or promotional use. For
information on bulk purchases please contact Macmillan Corporate and Premium Sales
Department at (800) 221-7945 x5442 or by email at specialmarkets@macmillan.com.

First edition 2015
Book design by Elliot Kreloff
Printed in the United States of America by Worzalla, Stevens Point, Wisconsin

10 9 8 7 6 5 4 3 2 1

Photo facing title page: Motown founder Berry Gordy, Jr., held fast to his musical dream.

For Amy

CONTENTS

A Greeting from the Groove . 1

The Motor City 5

Handsome Dazzler 9

Got a Job 15

Dreaming Big
for Eight Hundred Dollars 23

The Motown Family 28

My Mama Told Me 33

Factory Rhythm 37

The C Circuit 43

Miss Manners 49

Cholly's Moves 55

Dancing in the Street 59

Wonder Kid 65

The Funk Brothers 70

Ugly Sightseeing 73

Sunshine on a Cloudy Day 79

The Sound of Young America 87

Singing Supreme 93

Family Drama 99

What's Going On 103

TCB, ABC, 1-2-3-4-5 113

New Directions 121

The Groove Goes On 127

Author's Note 130

Timeline 133

Selected Discography 139

On Screen 146

Source Notes 147

For Further Enjoyment 157

Acknowledgments 161

Photo Credits 162

Index 163

Facing page: Whenever Smokey Robinson, third from left, and his group, the Miracles, sang, they invited fans to come along on a musical journey.

"Every day I watched how a bare metal frame, rolling down the line would come off the other end, a spanking brand new car. . . . Maybe, I could do the same thing with my music. Create a place where a kid off the street could walk in one door, an unknown . . . and come out another door, a star."

—*Berry Gordy, Jr., Motown founder*

"We did not set out to make black music. We set out to make quality music that everyone could enjoy and listen to." —*Smokey Robinson, singer-songwriter*

"It was bigger than we thought it was gonna be . . . We could make the ants dance." —*Joe Hunter, band director, the Funk Brothers*

"Gordy had found the magic formula for crossover."

—*Dick Clark, television host*

"They were songs to dance to. March to. Fly to . . . Music, pure and simple . . . Full of promise and determination, unity and humanity."

—*Marvin Gaye, musician, recording artist*

Facing page: The Marvelettes shook it up good every time they graced a stage.

A GREETING
FROM THE GROOVE

YOU READY, CHILD? LET'S GO.

I've got my pulse on all the roads. And side streets. And avenues. And alleyways.

You see, I steer the beat. That's why they call me the Groove.

Because my *uh-huh* keeps us pumping on the way. So—*uh-huh*, I'm the one driving this Rhythm Ride. Make no mistake, kid. I'm not a man or a woman. I'm a *guide*. A tempo that keeps us on track.

Hey, put that road map away. We don't need it. I know this highway. I'm clear on where I'm going—and I sure know where I've been. When you've lasted as long as I have, you learn that yesterday sets the path to today. Our past shows us where we've come from and where we're heading. The truth of it is, the Groove has been at the wheel for the whole time. That's why nobody can run me off the road. I'm here to stay. And now, I'd like to take *you* on a drive.

Yeah, you. Sitting pretty. Taking in the whole view from your window.

Make sure you stay alert, 'cause this Rhythm Ride is a trip—and a story about cars and stars, and a *sound*. It's the journey of one man's dream. That man, Berry Gordy, Jr., was an unstoppable originator. This is the true tale of how he took kids from the street and turned them into celebrities. Our drive follows Berry's vision-come-to-life. Honey, you're about to see how Berry's company put pride on the flip side of prejudice, and came to be called the Sound of Young America.

As we get ready to roll, you need to know something about the Groove. I'm blacker than midnight. And proud *of* it.

I've been pumped, sung, shunned, loved, let loose, danced to, segregated, and celebrated. I've driven *to* the beat and *through* it.

I've been called some names, too. Some good names—"praise tempo" and "heart-and-soul harmony."

And other names that put some painful scratches on my shiny black vinyl—names like "race music" and "darkie sounds."

Yeah, I've seen good days and bad.

Highs.

Lows.

In-betweens.

But I'm tough. I've got grit, deep down. I don't ever give up. I've stood the test of time.

Sweetie, before we get started, I need to warn you. There are happy places along this road and sad ones, too. Every time I take a kid on this ride, they come home changed. Different. Rhythm has a way of doing that. It stirs you up, then sets you down on higher ground.

You think you can handle it? *Good.*

Stick with the Groove.

Here we go

On a Rhythm Ride.

To a place.

Called Motown.

3

THE MOTOR CITY

BUCKLE UP, BABY. SETTLE IN.

Our trip begins with Berry Gordy, Jr., a kid who always kept his motor running. Berry lived with his family in Detroit, Michigan. In the late 1920s, when he was born, Detroit was a boomtown for African Americans. "The Motor City" was what folks called the sidewalks and streets that wove together their community. Detroit's pulse got its beat from the Ford Motor Company, the automotive industry's biggest employer of black men and women, and the only company that had come to an agreement with the United Auto Workers that prohibited discrimination based on race or skin color.

When someone new came to town, they immediately went to Ford to get a job. If a child was born in Detroit, people joked that the baby bounced from Henry Ford Hospital to the Ford Motor Company assembly belt, where he or she

Facing page: Detroit was an industrial city that attracted African American workers from the South who came to the North in search of jobs. As one of the world's largest automotive centers, Detroit offered opportunities for joining the ranks of men and women employed in what some called the "car capital."

The Ford Motor Company provided jobs to anyone willing to spend long hours on an assembly line building cars from the wheels up. The work was boring, but provided decent wages. African Americans and white people often worked side by side putting together car parts, though in some towns they were segregated.

would spend the rest of his or her days shaping fenders, tweaking headlights, or slapping car doors onto hot-off-the-line Model 59s.

Ford paid higher salaries than any other automotive company. At Ford, workers had the widest range of job opportunities. You could start as a welder and work your way up to foreman. There were many who took great pride in working at Ford and liked the camaraderie found on the assembly line.

But being employed by Ford wasn't all sparkling hubcaps and happy car horns. For some, making cars could be grueling. From morning to night, workers spent hours doing the same tasks again and again, with only two fifteen-minute breaks a day.

It went like this:

Stand . . . snatch . . . bend . . . attach . . .
Stand . . . snatch . . . bend . . . attach . . .

Also, the place was loud. It smelled like sweat and chrome polish. The bright lights made it hot. If you were lucky enough to be stationed near one of the small windows, there was no time to take even a quick look outside. For many folks, the paycheck made the long days and stale air bearable. But for others, it was tedious grunt work, not worth the money.

Berry's parents, Berry Gordy, Sr., and Bertha, owned a few successful businesses, which meant they didn't have to work for Ford. They were entrepreneurs who took pride in running their family establishments, and they taught their children the value of hard work.

Berry's father was a professional carpenter and plasterer. He also operated the Booker T. Washington General Store, his own grocery store named after the noted educator. And he was the owner of a local printing shop called Gordy Printing Shop.

Berry's mother cofounded the Friendship Mutual Life Insurance Company, a small business whose primary purpose was to provide affordable insurance policies to African American families.

As soon as the Gordy children were old enough to help their dad mix plaster or carry wood planks for his carpentry jobs, or stock shelves at their family grocery store, or hoist stacks of paper at the Gordy Printing Shop, or answer the phone at their mom's insurance company, they were put to work.

Berry's sisters, Loucye, Esther, Anna, and Gwen, and his brothers, Fuller, George, and Robert, went along with their family's way of doing things. They were focused students who brought home good grades and worked in their parents' establishments with little complaint.

Berry, Jr., the next-to-youngest child, wasn't like his siblings. He hated manual labor. He worked in his parents' businesses, but he did it with an attitude.

Berry didn't like how plastering got his hands dirty. Working with wood gave him splinters. Stacking cans of peas and piles of paper was boring.

Schoolwork for Berry was the same—misery.

When it came time for the Gordy kids to show their parents their report cards, Berry wasn't so eager to share what looked like a tribute to the fourth and sixth letters of the alphabet. Berry's parents weren't happy about his grades, but the Ds and Fs didn't come as a surprise to them, either.

Berry was a cutup in school and at home and was known as a troublemaker. When the teacher sat down at her desk, then couldn't get up because someone had smeared a puddle of glue on her chair, all eyes looked at Berry.

Or when a plastic worm floated in some unsuspecting student's noodle soup, the hungry kid would shout, "Gordy did this!" Berry's childhood motto was "No gag too big, no laugh too small."

But not everybody thought Berry's jokes were funny. He soon got a reputation as "Berry the bother."

And oh, was Berry's head big. He was shorter than even some of the girls in his grade but was the cockiest kid in school, with enough confidence to fill a hot-air balloon.

Even as a student who flunked most of his classes and spent lots of time in the principal's office for bad behavior, Berry was as ambitious as the rest of his family. He knew what it meant to be your own boss, and he knew he had a certain kind of smarts that would make him successful someday.

As we roll on, take a good look at this city, kid. It's pretty, right? And while you're looking, listen too, 'cause Detroit is a place that pulsates with possibility.

HANDSOME DAZZLER

GLAD OUR WINDSHIELD IS CLEAN, CHILD.

Because, like Berry Gordy, we have lots to view up ahead.

Berry had several passions. He liked jazz, dancing, and boxing. And he *loved* making money.

By the time he was a teenager, he had claimed his family's entrepreneurial tradition the way a quick-fingered kid grabs on to a carousel's brass ring, slips it past his fattest knuckle, and enjoys the rest of the ride in style. Young Berry was shrewd. He kept working for his parents, but instead of grumbling about what a pain in the neck it was, he started to pay close attention to how his mother and father ran their companies, kept track of their earnings, and brought in new customers. When he was still a kid, Berry started to build his own small businesses. He borrowed some of his dad's lumber and constructed his own shoeshine stand.

In a bold move, he sold the *Michigan Chronicle*, an African American-themed newspaper, in Detroit's all-white neighborhoods. He believed that since white people often hung out in black nightclubs, they'd be interested in reading about African American culture.

This was Berry's first glimpse into what would become the hallmark of his fortune—offering black culture to white consumers. Berry's newspaper sales were successful. The venture showed young Berry that he had good instincts about what customers wanted.

Drawing on his interest in music, Berry came up with an idea to launch his own door-to-door singing business. He decided on the songs, promoted the service, and scheduled the appointments. He hired a friend to sing the songs.

Right away, Berry started to experience what it was like to bring in cash from an idea that he'd generated. This was a great feeling.

Soon Berry could be seen around town at dance halls and jazz clubs, where the money he'd earned flew from his wallet as fast as a flock of eager pigeons escape a coop.

Berry always managed to hold on to some of his earnings, though, so that he could pursue another one of his interests—amateur boxing at Detroit's Brewster Center, a hangout for tough teens who dared to go into the ring. Berry had been inspired by Joe Louis, a famous African American boxer, who in 1937 became the heavyweight champion of the world. Joe, known as the Brown Bomber, had learned to fight in Detroit. Joe was a national hero whose boxing had earned him big bucks. Berry wanted to be like Joe. He had the skill and the drive to do it, too. In 1945, when Berry was sixteen, he dropped out of school to spend all his time training to become a boxing champion. This was a big ambition for a teenager who was small for his age.

Berry was good in the ring. Strategic. Strong. A focused fighter. But his family had its doubts about his ability to become a champ. So did the other athletes who trained at Brewster. This made Berry even more determined. When he put on his boxing gloves, he focused on Joe Louis's successes. Over a period of years, Berry won ten out of fifteen professional fights and showed all the doubters and nonbelievers that he wasn't playing around. He was there to win.

While training at Brewster, boxers often listened to the radio that spilled its music into the training hall. The music made Berry eager to pursue his desire to write songs. When he wasn't training for a fight, Berry had a pen and notepad in his hands and was making up song lyrics. During his boxing career, Berry fought a guy named Jackie Wilson, a singer who shared Berry's dream of someday making it big in the music business.

One day at the boxing gym, Berry was tired, bruised, achy. It was August and hotter than the hinges on the devil's front door. Berry noticed two posters stuck on a pillar at the gym. One poster was an ad for an upcoming contest between musical bands. The other poster advertised a boxing match that was happening at the same time.

Berry stared at both posters. The fighters in the photo that advertised the boxing match looked worn out. They weren't much older than Berry, but they had old age written all over their faces.

The band leaders on the other poster were handsome and smiling, ready to impress their listeners.

For Berry, staring at the two posters was like gazing into a crystal ball that predicted what his future might hold. He didn't want to turn into a haggard, hiney-whipped fighter. He saw himself as a handsome dazzler, not a washed-up

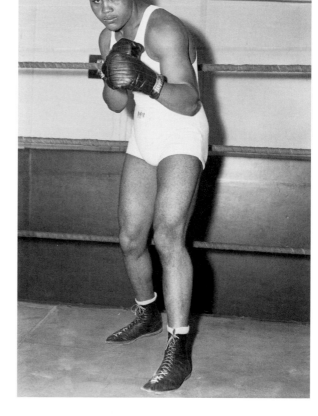

Boxing champ Joe Louis brought pride to African Americans, especially Berry Gordy. Joe was known for his pounding punches and fierce fighting. He was one of the most noted American athletes of his time.

boxer. Even with his track record in the ring, it didn't take Berry long to decide to hang up his boxing gloves to pursue songwriting full time.

Berry figured that one way to attract more customers to his family's print shop would be through music. He wrote a one-minute commercial jingle for the Gordy Print Shop and recorded the song in the basement studio of a local disc jockey. The song worked. With just sixty seconds of catchy music and lyrics that stayed locked in people's minds, more folks in the neighborhood came into the Gordy Print Shop *singing Berry's song.*

They browsed the shelves of the store *singing Berry's song.*

They purchased their merchandise and left the shop *singing Berry's song.*

This encouraged Berry to write his first full-length song, "You Are Loved," a ballad that was inspired by the film actress Doris Day. He spent twenty-five dollars to get the song published so that he could send a copy of the sheet music to the film star with a letter. (Doris Day didn't write back to Berry, but forty-three years after he'd written the song, Doris was happy to accept an invitation to meet with Berry Gordy so that he could present her with a framed copy of "You Are Loved.")

In 1951, Berry left Detroit to serve as a soldier in the Korean War, a conflict between North and South Korea. The war began in June 1950, when North Korea invaded South Korea. A few days later, President Harry S. Truman convinced the United Nations to send American military troops to the aid of South Korea.

Berry didn't want to go, but by law, he had to. He even tried to get out of serving by purposely flunking the IQ test they handed out at the military induction center. But too many of Berry's answers were correct, and he was forced to enlist.

After serving time in Korea, Berry returned to Detroit in 1953. Berry's father and his brother George loaned him

When Berry Gordy wrote the song "You Are Loved," he mailed it to Doris Day's home address in Hollywood, hoping the actress and singer would agree to record it. Doris had starred in several movie musicals and had recorded many records. Berry waited months for a response, but never got one. When he and Doris met years later, she told Berry that she'd never received his letter. They'd both become big celebrities by then.

money to open a record shop called 3-D Record Mart, which sat on the same block of buildings where the Booker T. Washington General Store and the Gordy Print Shop stood. Each of these buildings was owned by the Gordy family. Some people called the street they occupied "Gordy Strip."

Berry stocked the 3-D Record Mart shelves with mostly jazz recordings. He had come to love jazz during his days of hanging out in Detroit nightspots. But times had changed since then. Jazz wasn't as popular as rhythm and blues, a new form of music folks called R&B. On nights after closing up his record store, Berry sometimes passed groups of kids gathered on corners singing R&B under street-lights. This music's urban doo-wop spread its harmonies into the city streets, inviting neighbors to throw open their windows to let the doo-wops and croons fly into their living rooms.

It wasn't just the night owl neighbors who sang along with those kids. It seems every moth, lightning bug, and cricket joined the rhythm. They were no longer jamming to jazz. Their wings wanted to doo-wop.

Berry was forced to close his record store just two years after it opened. He learned that in business, it wasn't all about what Berry wanted. Success came with giving people what *they* wanted. By 1953, people grooved to rhythm and blues.

R&B was a soulful sound that put its arms around listeners and rocked them, sometimes gently, other times with a sure sway. It was popular in cities across America. But like many aspects of life in the United States, R&B wasn't free to roam where it pleased. This was a time in America when segregation laws prevented black students and white students from attending the same public schools. When drinking fountains and restaurants wore signs that said "Colored" and "Whites Only." When movie theaters and hotels didn't let black customers past the front door.

The same was true for R&B. Prejudice tried to keep it out. Hold it back.

Limit its soul-rousing power. Rhythm and blues was called "race music"—songs meant only for black singers and black listeners.

As R&B's popularity started to spread, it was kids who first realized that the concept behind race music made no sense. Rhythm doesn't have a color—it just has a beat. And the blues, well, everybody gets the blues.

Berry understood the appeal of R&B. He started to like it as much as he enjoyed jazz, especially when he saw its potential to break free of the race music fence that was keeping rhythm and blues from reaching the largest possible audience.

Seems like our road just got wider somehow, doesn't it, child? That always happens in these parts of the Rhythm Ride. Maybe that's because right around now Berry decided that his route to making big money was through music.

Though he'd closed his record store, Berry's desire to succeed as a business owner in some aspect of music was as wide open as ever.

GOT A JOB

NO, KID, THAT'S NOT THE GROOVE HUMMING.

What you feel is our ride ready to embrace the pace of what comes next. The same was true for Berry. By the time he was twenty-four, he was eager to shift gears. But it took him some time to get ahead.

Before the 3-D Record Mart shut down, Berry married nineteen-year-old Thelma Coleman, a medical worker who sometimes came into his shop. The couple had three children soon after they married. This forced Berry to get a job that brought in a steady paycheck and would allow him to support his family. There was one place Berry knew would hire him immediately. It was a place he'd avoided. But now, as a father, he had little choice but to take a job on the assembly line at the Ford Motor Company's Lincoln-Mercury automotive plant.

Lincoln-Mercury. It sounded impressive. A president and a planet. But, as Berry knew before taking the job, the work wasn't much to brag about. Berry was used to calling his own shots. Now he had to stand at a moving conveyor belt that served up auto frames, one after another, and fasten chrome strips and upholstery to the metal. Each week he took home $86.40. He supplemented his income by working weekends at Ford.

Man, it was drudgery. From the time Berry got to the factory each morning until he left at night, all he saw were car parts and other men like him who were stuck doing this kind of labor to make ends meet. All he heard was the noise of the assembly line—a rolling monster that let loose an endless groan that sounded like a sick man clearing his throat.

Berry escaped the grinding, mind-numbing work by filling his thoughts with ideas for new songs. But he was also noticing something that would help him in the future. He was learning the value of the assembly line. The Ford Motor Company had figured out that you could produce a lot of something that a lot of people wanted, and that this could be done quickly, over and over again.

Cars were built part by part. After each piece was put together, painted, and polished, the whole shiny automobile rolled off the assembly line ready to drive. Coming quickly behind it was another new car, just as sparkling and ready for some eager soul who couldn't wait to get behind its wheel.

Berry wondered if he could do this with his songs—create one glittering "model" after another that people were waiting for. If so, he could build a successful music business.

Berry quit his job at Ford. He told his wife that he planned to write songs full time. This didn't please Thelma. She wanted a husband who could put food on the table for their children. Thelma worried that Berry's pipe dreams couldn't pay the bills. She left her well-intentioned husband, and the couple divorced. Berry did his best to stay in touch with his children, though.

Berry moved in with his sister Gwen. During the day, he wrote songs, bought showy suits, and went to the barbershop to "get conked," a chemical process that straightened his cottony hair to make it smooth. He gained a reputation for being one of the prettiest boys in all of Detroit, with clothes folks called "flashy threads" and hair that was said to be "fried, dyed, and laid to the side."

At night, Berry hung out in local clubs where notable black singers such as Billie Holiday, Etta James, Sarah Vaughan, and Dinah Washington performed to packed houses. These singers knew just what to do to put the *blue* in *the blues* and the right rhythms in R&B. With their powerful singing voices, they could light the lows, vibrate the highs, scratch the backbeats, and bellow all the notes in-between. Berry watched the effect these singers had on their audiences, and saw how their music stirred black and white listeners equally. In many respects, their vocal abilities were transcending the confines of race music.

Berry's sisters Gwen and Anna owned a photo concession stand at one of the nightclubs. They knew many of the performers and were happy to introduce their brother Berry whose hip clothes, conked hair, broad smile, and winning charm had an immediate appeal. Berry started writing songs for the performers he'd met. He became a songwriter-for-hire, which meant he created a tune and got a set amount of cash for his work. One of his first successes was a song called "All I Could Do Was Cry," which was sung by Etta James and became a hit.

In 1957, Berry co-wrote a song called "Reet Petite" that was sung by Jackie Wilson, his buddy from the boxing ring. By this time, Jackie had become a popular singer. When Jackie belted Berry's tune, people stopped what they were doing and listened. "Reet Petite" was Berry's first song to top the music charts. He then wrote two more songs for Jackie. They also became hits and established Berry as a talented songwriter who knew what it took to create sellable music.

Berry Gordy's good looks, charm, and smarts helped open doors that led to opportunities for hobnobbing with famous singers who inspired him as a songwriter.

Jackie Wilson, Berry Gordy's boxing buddy, started performing in Detroit nightclubs when he was sixteen. He was a talented singer and performer whose nickname was "Mr. Excitement" because of the way he put his own special sizzle on a tune. When Jackie rolled out the "Oh! Ah!" refrain of Berry's "Reet Petite," it made kids sing along, and sent that song to the top of the music charts.

Berry's songs earned hundreds of thousands of dollars. But as a writer-for-hire, Berry received very little of this money. His small one-time writer's fee didn't include royalty income, which was additional money earned each time a record was sold or one of Berry's songs was played on the radio.

Instead, most of the money went to the record companies, which were mostly white-owned. These rich executives grew richer from the money Berry's songs brought in.

Berry's bank account dwindled as all his money went to paying his bills. He was considered one of the hottest songwriters in all of Detroit. But his music had brought him quick cash, not lasting profits.

No matter how successful Berry's songs were, they didn't pay him enough to keep his boiler running on cold winter nights, or afford a good meal.

"Hot" Berry was stone-cold broke.

The same was true for the black singers and musicians who performed the songs. They put their hearts, souls, voices, grit, and guts into their vocals, but the payment terms under which they worked were unfair. The white record companies controlled all the rights to the music. Black talent *made* the songs, but white businessmen *owned* them.

Images of black singers were sometimes considered unattractive by white-owned record companies. Some of the white record producers believed that showing Jackie Wilson's or Etta James's picture on the cover of a record was a deterrent that would prevent white people from buying it.

This was especially true in the segregated South, where African Americans were treated as second-rate citizens, and where white teenagers, who were often buying the records, didn't want their parents to know they were enjoying music sung by black people.

Record companies often "white washed" the covers of records. Sometimes recordings of songs that were sung by black people showed white people on record covers. Or, a record cover would show an image such as a beach or sunset scene that included no people. Not only did black performers get little money, they also got no recognition.

Berry was sick of seeing his hard-earned creativity and the talents of black performers go unrewarded. He began to seriously consider building a record label that would allow him to produce the work of black artists, to publish his music, to have complete control over the money he and the singers earned, and also to have control over how black performers were portrayed to the public.

Berry's sister Gwen shared Berry's vision of creating a record label. Having worked in nightclubs with many of the singers Berry had written songs for, and having grown up with the business smarts of the Gordy family, Gwen understood what was required to become a successful entrepreneur. She launched Anna Records, a label named after their sister. Gwen invited Berry to join her business. But Berry wasn't a joiner or a follower. And he didn't much like sharing. What he *did* like was being his own boss—and being *the* boss of those who worked with him.

For Berry, this wasn't about greed. It was about love. Any mama or daddy will do what's needed to protect those they love, especially their children. Songwriting was like that for Berry. He had brought his songs into this world. He had nurtured them and raised them up. Berry loved his songs the way a father loves his own children. They were part of him.

He was ready to do what was needed to protect his songs. That's why Berry was so dead set on keeping his business all to himself—to make sure everything was done fairly, and that his artists were treated well and earned the money they were entitled to.

They say conviction is the first step to greatness. Well, Berry Gordy had the conviction of ten men. He also had a knack for knowing the kinds of songs and entertainers that would appeal to the most people. He could sniff out a hit quicker than a hungry kid could smell cookies baking.

Building a business takes time and money. Now that Berry wasn't reporting to a job at Ford, he could work whenever he wanted, taking his own sweet time perfecting songs.

But he didn't have the funds he needed to get his company started right away. To launch her record label, his sister Gwen had spent years saving the money she'd earned from her photo concession stand. Berry didn't have any savings.

Berry continued to write music that he sold to major record labels that produced and published the songs, and, therefore, he wasn't entitled to receive payments after the songs were released to the public.

But Berry became smarter about asking for more money up front, even though the companies still controlled the royalties, the money earned from the number of records sold.

In 1957, when Berry was twenty-eight, he had one of the most important meetups in his career.

Berry was hanging out in the office of Nat Tarnopol, a music producer who had worked with singer Jackie Wilson. On this day, four guys and a girl who called themselves the Matadors came in to audition for Nat. At the audition, these kids sang like tomorrow would never come. They gave it all they had. Nat wasn't impressed. He shooed them off midway through their third song.

But Berry saw something special in the group, especially in the lead singer, whose voice had a unique quality to it. This kid's singing was sweeter than apple pie, made with some kind of secret brown-sugar recipe. He was handsome, too, with butterscotch skin, green eyes, and a smile that went on for miles.

Berry was also taken with the group's musical arrangements and lyrics. As the teens started to leave, Berry chased after them. When he introduced himself, the lead singer recognized Berry's name right away as the creator of Jackie Wilson's "To Be Loved" and "Reet Petite." This also impressed Berry, who asked the kids for the name of the person who had written their songs.

That's when the lead singer, seventeen-year-old William "Smokey" Robinson, introduced himself to Berry. He showed Berry his school notebook filled with song lyrics he'd written in pencil. Berry asked Smokey to sing his favorite one. It was a song about love that, in Berry's opinion, needed work. Berry didn't hold back in offering Smokey some hard-core criticism, along with tips on how to improve the song.

Some aspiring songwriters might have been daunted by Berry's straightforwardness. Not Smokey. He was happy to get Berry's feedback and excited to work at developing his songs by putting Berry's advice into practice.

Smokey's determination and passion for music immediately struck Berry as the right attitude for a professional singer-songwriter. He sensed, too, that this talented performer had the potential to create songs that would be gobbled up by other kids. Also, Smokey was humble. And eager. Berry liked that. He and Smokey formed a friendship that would last decades. Together, they co-wrote a song called "Got a Job."

Berry came up with the idea to change the name of the Matadors to the Miracles. The original group consisted of Warren "Pete" Moore, Claudette Rogers Robinson, Bobby Rogers, Marv Tarplin, and Ronnie White.

On Smokey's eighteenth birthday, February 19, 1958, "Got a Job" was released. With that song, Smokey got more than a job. He got two of the best birthday gifts ever—a hit record and overnight stardom!

But Smokey and Berry's star couldn't shine as brightly as they'd hoped. As soon as the mailman arrived holding an envelope from the record company with what Berry hoped would be a fat royalty check, he ripped open the envelope to find a check for a measly $3.19!

For that amount of money, Berry could buy one gallon of milk for a dollar, six packs of gum for twenty cents, and five cans of tomato soup for fifty cents. That left him with $1.49, which wasn't a lot to spend on doing something enjoyable, considering how hard he'd worked to earn the money.

And eating tomato soup every night for dinner can get dull. Chomping on a bunch of Dubble Bubble tastes good, but it isn't decent payback for selling thousands of records that thousands of people were singing day and night and all the hours in-between.

Bubble gum is sweet when you first start to chew, but honey, after an hour the sweet is gone. That's what songwriting had become for Berry—a sweet sensation that didn't pay off in the end.

DREAMING BIG FOR
EIGHT HUNDRED DOLLARS

KID, WHEN MOST FOLKS MIGHT WANT TO QUIT SOMETHING, BERRY GORDY WAS JUST GETTING STARTED.

If someone else had been in Berry's shoes, they might have given up their dream of making music. After all, it was hard work. It was unpredictable. The chances of making it big were slim, and there were many obstacles to overcome.

Fortunately, the person in Berry Gordy's shoes was the determined Berry Gordy.

Yes, child, Berry Gordy, who was one of the most convincing people in town. Berry Gordy, who came from a family that could help him strive toward success.

So Berry called a family meeting. He walked up to the front door of his parents' home, rang the bell, stepped inside, smiled big. Made nice to everybody who'd gathered around the dining room table as he prepared to make his request.

Berry wasted no time. He put it to his family straight. He asked them for a loan of a thousand dollars from family savings to produce a record that would launch his own record company. This money was the entire Gordy nest egg that they'd set aside for emergencies. Berry reminded his family that he'd written songs for Jackie Wilson and Smokey Robinson. Berry's family *reminded him* that he had nothing to show for his efforts.

Berry told them that's exactly *why* he needed the money—so that he could create his own recording company that would give him something to show for all his hard work. Berry talked and talked and talked about his plans for building a record empire. He told his family how he would create a hit-making machine. He tried to convince them of his ability to succeed.

The Gordy family was reluctant. They discussed, debated, doubted. Berry's mother was the most cautious. Berry's sister Esther had been the one who'd managed the thousand dollars of family savings, and was not eager to clean out her family's money so that her younger brother could plunk it into an unknown venture.

Even more than the chewiest wad of Dubble Bubble, Berry's family stuck it to him:

What if this so-called hit-making machine fails?

Where will we be if the records flop?

How will you pay back our money?

Finally, after hours of conversation, the Gordys agreed to lend Berry eight hundred dollars. That was enough to get him started.

The loan from Berry's family gave Berry's dream the kick start it needed.

Berry purchased a two-story bungalow at 2648 West Grand Boulevard, in the heart of Detroit's black community. The white clapboard house with a large picture window in the front would serve as headquarters for Berry's company. It stood on a tree-lined street that offered plenty of shade, but also let the sun's rays play on the sidewalks.

Berry and his family hung a sign out front that immediately caught the attention of anyone who passed by. Neighbors looked at that sign and wondered what would come out of that house.

When young mothers wheeled their babies by in strollers, the toddlers who saw those bold blue letters did a double take.

Even dogs out for a walk and stray cats trying to find their way home took notice of Berry's sign.

It was a sign of the times.

It was Berry's make-no-mistake intention.

It said:

HITSVILLE U.S.A.

Detroit's West Grand Boulevard was home to several African American–owned businesses, including the bungalow that would serve as home to Berry Gordy's company, which he named "Hitsville U.S.A."

This was the name of the building that would house Berry's company. Berry's plan was to make only hits—songs that would drive straight to the top of the record charts.

No flops.

No middle-of-the-road music.

No fair-to-middling tunes.

To launch his dream, Berry drew on his experience working at the Ford Motor Company. His goal was to turn his record company into an assembly line that cranked out hit after hit after hit. Like he was putting together a beautiful car—or a flashy car, or a sports car, or any kind of car that someone was eager to own—Berry would take all the needed parts, assemble them piece by piece, polish them, and let each roll off his company's "assembly line" for customers who were quick to buy them.

Berry wasn't producing just any kind of record by any kind of singer. Tremendous thought, planning, and strategy went into building the talent that would become part of his venture's lineup.

Before officially opening, Berry organized his headquarters into several important units. The building's ground floor was converted into a lobby and control room. Berry divided the top floor into a music room, offices, and his living quarters. The dirt-floor garage became Studio A, where artists would record their music. On days when musicians, singers, instruments, and recording equipment filled the studio, it was cramped and hot. With microphone cords dangling from above, and everything packed in tight, they called the small, dark place "the snake pit."

Berry's family became company employees. His parents served as advisers for many aspects of the business. Esther, Berry's sister, and Esther's husband, George, an accountant, managed the finances. Berry's sister Loucye was in charge of manufacturing, billing, shipping, and graphic design for printed materials.

Berry's brother George produced songs. Robert ran the music publishing. Fuller oversaw the hiring.

The Gordy family funds were like a set of jumper cables that ignited power back into a stalled motor. Honey, Berry put that money to good use. He came up with a name for his company that sang the praises of Detroit—"the Motor City"—and also captured the hometown feeling of his roots.

He called his company *Motown*. It was 1959. The year this Groove started to make some smooth moves. Hitsville became Motown's nickname. It's what people often called Berry's company when they talked about it. Still do, child. Still do.

THE MOTOWN FAMILY

BERRY BUILT MOTOWN TO BE MORE THAN JUST A RECORD COMPANY.

To him, Motown was a family. Anyone who was brought in to work at the company, whether they were Berry's blood relatives or not, were considered members of "the Motown family."

And, child, there sure were a whole lot of aspiring singers who were eager to become sisters, brothers, or cousins on the Motown family tree. Hitsville U.S.A. had a small front yard that was often filled with kids from the neighborhood. They weren't out there playing tag or hide-and-seek. Those kids were bringing on their best game, rolling out tunes, doo-wopping, and slick-stepping dance moves that were smoother than smooth. More than anything, they wanted Berry Gordy to take notice. They wanted to be discovered by the man who had become the talk of Detroit. They hoped to be invited past the front door of Hitsville U.S.A., where records were being made.

The word on the street was simple. A singer who walked *in* to Motown an unknown had the potential to walk *out* a star. Also, Motown had a good reputation for being a nurturing environment, in which, like a family, members were supportive of one another's talents. Motown singers and employees enjoyed meals together, barbecued in the backyard, played cards, prayed together, and, of course, made music together.

Smokey Robinson, head of the singing group the Miracles, was one of the first singer-songwriters Berry employed at Motown. Smokey and the Miracles had proved their ability to create a hit with the success of their song "Got a Job."

Some kids didn't wait to be asked to come into Motown. They applied for

Hitsville's performers were like one big happy family. Here, Berry plays the piano while Motown's "brothers and sisters" have fun with a sing-along. This "family photo" was taken a few years after Motown became established.

jobs in the company. Every day a boy or girl showed up at Hitsville, ready to do any kind of work that might help them get a foot in the door. They'd offer to stack papers, open mail, sweep floors, or clean toilets. One teenager named Martha Reeves was lucky enough to be hired as Motown's receptionist. It was her job to greet people who came in off the street and to answer the telephone. Hoping she would get the chance to sing for Berry, Martha didn't just welcome visitors or answer the phone by *saying* hello.

Martha *sang* her greeting with a soprano voice that made people wonder, *Who's that girl?*

Even though Martha sang into the phone and not on a record, as a Motown employee, she was already a member of the Motown family, and she had a front-row seat to Berry's way of doing things as he grew Motown into a small corporation.

If you were a member of the Motown family, you had to follow the rules set forth by the man employees called "Mr. Gordy" or "Big Boss" or "B.G."

There was the No List and the Do List:

No acting up.

No wild partying.

No excessive drinking.

Absolutely *no* drugs.

Do respect one another.

Do conduct yourself with dignity.

Do praise fellow Motown family members.

Do have fun.

Berry encouraged his talent to try new ways of blending vocals. To experiment with melodies and song lyrics. To push past conventional bounds so the music that came out of Motown had its own distinct sound.

Staying true to his business model of running Motown like a car factory, Berry organized regular "quality control" meetings. These gatherings were to test songs before they went to market. In the same way automakers made sure cars included all the right components, that they had attributes that would appeal to the most customers, and that they *worked*, Berry put each and every Motown song to the test before he "rolled it out."

From his days as a boxer, Berry had learned that competition breeds champions. Quality-control meetings were fiercely competitive and, at the same time, were conducted in an atmosphere that fostered the nurturing of everybody's ideas.

At the Friday morning meetings, songwriters and producers would submit their songs for review. Berry would also present any songs and ideas he was working on, and everyone would vote for that meeting's winner. This was part of Berry's philosophy. Each songwriter was subject to a creative critique. Nobody was exempt from feedback, including "Big Boss."

Opinions from many areas of the Motown family were considered. The sales force had a say. The office help had a say. Secretaries had a say. The cleaning crew had a say. Singers had a say. On a summer day when the windows had been left open, if the flies and mosquitoes that found their way inside could have voiced an opinion, their buggy views also would have been taken under consideration.

Those meetings could bring on some heavy bickering. Songwriters and singers would go to battle for a ballad, claiming theirs was the best song of the day. Composers would fight about F-flats and whose falsetto was better. They'd attack a backbeat in a heartbeat. A lyricist or songwriter such as Smokey Robinson might come into the meeting riding high on the words of his new song, only to have somebody burst the bubble on what he thought was a golden lyric line.

Even Berry, who, when he was a kid, was the joke king, could be the brunt of somebody's snicker about a song he'd written. Some days, things got heated, with songwriters or vocalists facing off and claiming things such as, "Man, my song is better than yours!"

Fistfights weren't allowed, of course. But after hours of debate and competition, people could get tired.

That's when Berry would put it to a vote. Yes or no.

To help with the voting, he would ask the group, "If you only had a dollar in your pocket, and you were hungry, would you buy a hot dog or this record?"

The song that won out over the hungry man's hot dog was the winner and would be released to the public. These weekly meetings seemed to have some kind of magic formula associated with them. Really, it's true, child. No lie.

Motown was still in its early stages, but if a song was approved on a Friday morning, it had a good chance of becoming a hit.

MY MAMA TOLD ME

HONEY, THESE WERE GOOD TIMES.

Some of the best the Groove has ever seen. Soon Berry's vision of creating a record company structured like a car factory that mass-produced its products was coming to fruition. The experience he'd gained at the Lincoln-Mercury plant was beginning to pay off. Under Berry's creative direction, the assembly-line philosophy took on a whole new meaning. Now, instead of a president and a planet, the factory ideal represented power and possibility.

One aspect that made Motown even more appealing was that Berry treated black artists fairly. African Americans earned the profits they were entitled to.

To drive home this idea, Berry and a Motown employee, Janie Bradford, wrote a song called "Money (That's What I Want)."

It sounds kind of greedy, doesn't it, kid? I mean, lots of us want money, but how many go around singing about it?

But that's how Berry did things. He told it like it was. His songs expressed what we really felt inside. That's why his music appealed to people.

"Money" was recorded by Barrett Strong, a singer whose gutsy delivery of the song reminded everyone that while the best things in life are free, it sure is nice to have some cash.

Smokey Robinson (center) and the Miracles had all the right stuff—good looks, one-of-a-kind vocals, and teen appeal. Smokey was their songwriter and lead singer. Here, he's smiling pretty with, back left, Pete Moore; front left, Bobby Rogers; back right, Ronnie White; and front right, Claudette Robinson, Smokey's wife. Claudette Robinson left the group soon after it was formed.

After it was released in 1960, "Money" stayed in the Top 40 for eight weeks. Lots of folks could relate to the words of Motown's first big hit: "Your love gives me such a thrill / but your love don't pay my bills."

The sad thing is that "Money" didn't pay Berry's or Barrett's bills, either. Though the song became a hit, it had first been distributed locally, then nationally.

"Money" had garnered a lot of fame, but the two-part distribution *cost* a lot of money. Because "Money" had not been a national release from its beginning, the song didn't *earn* good money. What Berry did earn was a good lesson from the experience. After that, he considered all factors before releasing any song. He thought very carefully about the best ways to produce songs, record them, and distribute them to get to the widest possible audience.

On a Friday morning, Smokey Robinson went into a quality-control meeting excited to share his latest creation, a song titled "Shop Around." Smokey sang the slow, bluesy ballad for the group. There were aspects of the song that were appealing, but deep down Berry knew "Shop Around" needed something more. When the song was released in the fall of 1960, its sales were sluggish.

The lyrics, melody, and tempo of "Shop Around" kept Berry up at night. It was a song that seemed to have all the right ingredients—simple lyrics, a memorable concept, emotion—but it wasn't living up to Motown's quality-control promise of hit-making. One night "Shop Around" raced through Berry's thoughts, becoming a frenzied siren as he tried to sleep. Then it dawned on Berry. That's exactly what "Shop Around" needed. Some fire, some heat, a greater sense of urgency.

"Shop Around" wasn't meant to lull its listeners. It was meant to make people snap their fingers and sing along to its beat.

Berry got up and called Smokey at three o'clock in the morning. It was so dark outside and so early that even the *dew* didn't know what to *do*. Berry told Smokey to quickly gather the Miracles and to come to the recording studio at Hitsville U.S.A. They had a new record to make!

Smokey and the Miracles showed up half-awake, but when Berry started to play "Shop Around" on the piano, bringing it alive with an up-tempo beat, Smokey and his group caught on quick. They rearranged and re-recorded the song as a soul-bouncing R&B pop tune whose refrain makes you wanna stare down your mirror, wink at yourself, and sing your mama's warning loud enough to wake *her* mama from a deep sleep.

When the new version of the song was released, it sold a million copies in just a few months. It became Motown's first million-copy seller, soaring to the number-one spot on the *Billboard* magazine R&B chart, where it enjoyed a view from the top for eight weeks.

Are you good at math, kid? Yeah? Well then, maybe there's a future for you in tallying hits. To determine if a song makes it onto a *Billboard* chart, record sales and radio air play are tabulated in various music categories. The results are printed in *Billboard* magazine.

For any record to be named a gold record by the Recording Industry Association of America, it needs to sell 500,000 copies or more.

The Miracles' "Shop Around" had a groove-happy beat and sing-along lyrics that made kids wanna dance. Smokey and the Miracles showed how "Shop Around" could inspire a shuffle-step.

As a record that sold a million copies, "Shop Around" became Motown's first gold record.

White kids from suburbia shopped for "Shop Around." So did their parents. And when they found the record, they bought it. And they played it. And they told their friends to buy it, and *they* played it, too. And from Podunk to Parsippany, white kids sang along to black music.

The same was true for African American kids from inner cities and small towns who also shopped around for "Shop Around."

Their grandmas and grandpas and kid brothers and baby sisters all listened to that record. And they loved it. With "Shop Around" Berry had achieved crossover success. The skin color of Smokey Robinson and the Miracles didn't matter to listeners.

Black folks and white folks from all parts of the country played the record till those vinyl discs were cut with grooves so deep that it made me proud.

FACTORY RHYTHM

STOP FOR GAS? NO, CHILD.

This ride is fully pumped. My beat has all the fuel we need. Besides, we've got a lot more driving to do. Can't slow down now. No. *Uh-uh*.

As we speed up, here's something important that you need to understand. One aspect of Motown songs that made them stick inside people's minds was that each of them told a story. Most of the stories were about love—wanting love, waiting for love, finding love, being loved, saying hello to love, or kissing love good-bye. The big, early Motown hits conveyed simple human emotions that made you feel what those lyrics were saying.

The recipe for success for Motown's songs sounds simple. But only the Motown family's growing roster of songwriters, producers, and performers knew how to sprinkle each song with just the right ingredients to make its juices really *sing*.

"Shop Around" was a good example of Motown's mojo. Soon after "Shop Around" made it to the top of the *Billboard* chart, things started to accelerate at Hitsville U.S.A.

When people passed 2648 West Grand Boulevard, it was like taking a stroll past a factory. Outside, the place looked like other houses on the block, but behind Hitsville's sign, Motown's assembly line began turning out hits in quick succession. And the company was geared up for a whole bunch of hit-cranking. It was as if Berry's neighbors could hear engines humming, pistons hissing, and a chassis waxer putting polish on a gleaming machine. But that factory rhythm wasn't about making cars. It was about making *stars*.

Hitsville was the house that never slept. Recording and songwriting sessions often lasted all night long and kept going into the next day. The musicians didn't live at Hitsville, but they sometimes slept over or took naps between late takes.

When Mary Wells was in middle school, she spent her spare time helping her mother earn money as a housekeeper. Her wish was to go from splashing Spic and Span to singing—a dream that came true when she was signed at Motown, where her vocals were shinier than a fresh-mopped floor.

The ones who were best prepared for crack-of-dawn creativity made sure they always had a spare toothbrush and an extra pair of underwear handy. If Berry had wanted to hang another sign out front, it could have said: "Open 24 Hours." Motown's heated quality-control debates, group rehearsals, and late-night recording sessions sent Hitsville's R&B into the Detroit streets.

Following the success of the Miracles' "Shop Around," Motown introduced a nineteen-year-old vocalist named Mary Wells. Mary had grown up in Detroit, where, as a kid, she sometimes went to work with her mother, who was a cleaning lady. Mary hated scrubbing floors, but by helping her mother, she was also helping her family earn a living. To get through the grueling work, Mary sang songs she'd learned as a member of the church choir. By age twelve, she was performing in Detroit nightclubs on weekends and during summers when school wasn't in session.

After graduating from high school, Mary decided to pursue a full-time career as a singer and songwriter. In 1960, when Mary was seventeen, she spotted Berry Gordy at Detroit's 20 Grand nightclub and pleaded with him to let her share a song she'd written called "Bye, Bye, Baby." Mary knew of Berry's success with Motown. She had written the song with Jackie Wilson in mind as the one who could best sing it.

Berry was busy working the crowd at the nightclub, but Mary would not leave him alone. She begged for just a moment of his time. Finally, rather than keep on begging, Mary started singing in her soulful, raspy voice. Berry was impressed. He agreed to meet with Mary at the Motown offices the next day. She sang her song for Berry, this time without interruptions from the night-club noise.

In time, Berry signed Mary at Motown and paired her with Smokey Robinson. Though Mary's childhood work as a housekeeper was far behind her, she could put a high shine on a song. Like Berry, Smokey recognized Mary's talent and the unique qualities in her voice. Her sultry singing style inspired Smokey to write songs for her, and by 1962, when you turned on your radio, you could hear Mary Wells singing the hits Smokey had created. "The One Who Really Loves You," "You Beat Me to the Punch," and "Two Lovers" each topped the musical charts.

But the Motown engine was just revving up. In 1964, Mary recorded a song titled "My Guy," written and produced by Smokey Robinson.

"My Guy" is about dedication, child. It's about commitment. Guys and girls wailed the words to "My Guy" as an anthem about the one you love, or the one who loves you. It was an instant hit.

The Marvelettes had big voices, big smiles, and big hairdos. They were high school classmates who became one of Motown's first girl groups.

Guys imagined girls singing the song to express their devotion to them. Girls sang the song to let everybody know that they were committed to one very special guy and that nothing could come between a girl and her boyfriend.

When Mary Wells sang "My Guy," she enjoyed the quiet satisfaction of knowing that whoever happened to be *her* guy was a man committed to a woman who, because of her status as Motown's first solo superstar, had become recognized as "The First Lady of Motown."

When Berry had first met Mary Wells and seen her potential as a solo vocalist, he'd started to wonder—if one female singer could possibly capture the attention of the public, perhaps a *group* of women singers could also make people stop and listen, and sing along.

As Mary was just beginning her career at Motown, Berry was visiting local high schools to check out their talent shows and choruses, combing the city of Detroit for a female ensemble. One evening, Berry slid into a hard auditorium seat at Inkster High School, where the curtain was about to go up on the Inkster High talent night. As soon as Katherine Anderson, Juanita Cowart, Georgia Dobbins, Gladys Horton, and Georgeanna Tillman started to sing, Berry knew *this* was the hot female group he needed to add to Motown's roster.

The teens called themselves the Marvelettes, and they sure *were* a marvel! These high school students had brains, beauty, and stage appeal. And, like Berry, they knew what kinds of songs other teens wanted.

Berry allowed the girls to audition for Motown. To audition, they needed an original song. Georgia Dobbins got a blues song from her friend, a songwriter named William Garrett. It was a song about a girl waiting by the mailbox for a letter to come from a special boy. In just one night, Georgia reworked the song to showcase the talent of her singing group. Their group's rendition—which included backup vocals and also showed the range of voices among the five singers—persuaded Berry to sign the group.

Before the Marvelettes recorded the song for Motown, it was reworked again by Motown singer-songwriters Brian Holland and Robert Bateman, who turned it into a catchy ode to the mailman and called it "Please Mr. Postman."

Georgia left the group before the Marvelettes officially signed with Motown. But the song Georgia wrote became a million-copy seller.

In 1961, "Please Mr. Postman" became Motown's first number one *Billboard* Hot 100 pop-single chart hit. This placement was on a whole other hit-list that is different from the R&B charts where many of Motown's previous songs enjoyed success. And, sweetie, for teens who loved to croon that tune, hanging out by the mailbox waiting for you-know-who to arrive with a card or letter got to be more popular than meeting up at the soda shop for an egg cream.

THE C CIRCUIT

IT'S ONE THING TO HEAR MUSIC PLAYED ON A RECORD.

But, honey, it's another to *see* the ones doing the singing.

To *see* them perform live.

To *see* them up close.

To *watch* their lips rounding the notes.

To witness their hips swaying to the beat of music you know down in your own bones, because you've listened to it at least a million and three times.

Berry believed that if fans were coming to Motown's music through buying records, they'd come out in crowds to experience the music performed in front of them. He also figured that giving teens something to *see* would entice them to buy more records every time an artist they'd watched perform released a new song in the future. Berry thought that the memory of having set your eyes on a

Facing page: It was Berry's idea to send his artists on the road. The Motortown Revue allowed fans to see the stars whose music they'd been singing to. This sparked future record sales. By attending live performances, teens felt they'd "met" singers such as the Marvelettes, shown here, and wanted to buy music by these superstars to preserve the memories of seeing them in concert.

Traveling shows that included multiple artists took weeks to plan. Left to right, members of the Motown family, Maurice King, Billy Davis, Marvin Gaye, and Harvey Fuqua chart the details for a road show that will feature the Miracles.

singer smiling at the audience, expressing a song through dance moves, or wincing while singing a song's saddest parts would form a greater impression on listeners than having only heard a song being sung on a record or the radio.

Touring wasn't a new concept. During the 1950s, rock-and-roll singers frequently went on the road to perform in small towns and cities. These shows were often arranged by deejays—the people who worked at radio stations and chose which records would be played on the air—and the singers themselves. They could sometimes be disorganized and didn't function with a unified purpose.

The deejays were focused on gaining radio listeners. The performers were focused on increasing fans. The record companies had very little involvement in arranging the tours. They counted on the exposure to sell more records but didn't have a hand in pulling the acts together.

Berry approached the concept differently. He decided to *invest* in a tour. He conceived of a traveling show of which he oversaw all aspects. Motown was the first record company in history to market artists by sending them on the road for the purpose of developing "tour support."

One morning in October 1962, Detroit stood under a warm sky. Berry waited out front at Hitsville U.S.A. to help his singers prepare for the Motortown Revue, a ten-week tour of America.

Berry would not accompany them throughout the tour but would meet up with the caravan in select cities to check on their progress, to observe how his artists were received by audiences, and to see how they were holding up under the pressures of nonstop performing and traveling.

On that autumn morning, a bus and five cars were parked along West Grand Boulevard, waiting for Motown headliners Smokey Robinson and the Miracles, Mary Wells, and the Marvelettes to pile in.

Also joining the tour would be several musicians and some of Motown's up-and-coming performers. These included a singing group known as the Contours, and a shy newcomer named Marvin Gaye, who was married to Berry's sister Anna. Martha Reeves, who was still serving as a secretary at Motown, was invited along, too. She had formed a singing group called the Vandellas, which had signed with Motown in 1962 but had not yet had a Motown hit. This tour would give them the chance to try out their songs on audiences.

Child, you should have seen those kids pushing and shoving to get onto that bus and into those cars. You would have thought they were traveling to some kind of promised land. Many of them hadn't been but a few miles outside of Detroit, and now they were on their way to the Howard Theatre in Washington, D.C., where the Motortown Revue would make its debut. To them, the opportunity to sing and play music in front of live audiences *was* a kind of promise that signaled the beginning of a new day in their careers as performers.

From Washington, they would perform one night only in a series of select cities in the South, then head north for a ten-day gig at the Apollo Theater in New York City's Harlem, the place known as the capital of black America, a hotbed of African American life and culture.

Harlem's Apollo Theater, a popular night-spot in the center of New York City's "black mecca," was considered the pinnacle of showbiz success. When Motown's performers graced its stage, they were met with big applause.

The Apollo, Harlem's most notable performance hall, was *the* place where black talent could shine brightest. If you were black and could make it at the Apollo, then you were black and golden at the same time.

But before the Motortown Revue reached Harlem's sparkling streets, the travelers had to pass through the segregated South. In Detroit, African Americans and white people often worked side by side at the Ford Motor Company and in other places, so most of Berry's performers hadn't yet experienced the ugliest aspects of prejudice. Also, these kids existed in a kind of Motown celebrity bubble. Some naively considered themselves singing stars immune to the degradation of the Jim Crow laws that kept black people and white people separate in public places.

When the Motortown Revue tour bus and cars pulled into the parking lot of a southern hotel or restaurant, they were met with signs that said "Whites Only" or "No Coloreds." In the South, the performers sometimes had to sleep on their bus, or depend on the kindness of African American townspeople who would put them up for the night.

Once, after performing in Birmingham, Alabama, for a racially mixed audience, the singers and musicians—who had grown accustomed to standing ovations—were met with gunshots fired at their tour bus as they drove off with a swell of dirt and dust rising behind them. In the flurry, they had no way of knowing if the gunshots were being fired by audience members they had just performed for or if the shooting was coming from racist people who were waiting outside for them.

Up north, things were better, but in some ways still degrading. The Motortown Revue was very well received at mostly black clubs on what folks called "the chitlin circuit."

Kid, have you ever sniffed chitlins bubbling in a pot on the stove? Have you ever slurped down some chitlins?

When people want to talk proper, they call 'em by their correct name—*chitterlings*. That makes them sound so dainty. Like some kind of puff-pastry dusted in sugar. If you say *chitterlings* slowly, with a stuffy accent and a turned-up nose, you could pass them off as a treat at a tea party.

But, baby, the truth is, *chitterlings*—or chitlins when you're in familiar company—are hog intestines that were sometimes referred to in association with African Americans.

I'll tell you this. There are some good things about chitlins. If you like to chew a lot, they're very rubbery. Also, some would argue that chitlins are high in protein, and can be part of a balanced diet. But no matter how you slice 'em, slurp 'em, or say their name, chitlins are slimy swine innards that have a stinky smell.

So while the Motown performers were pleased to travel to a series of African American theaters that welcomed them, some found the term "chitlin circuit" demeaning.

Berry was determined to see his performers go beyond what was called "the *C* circuit." The performances at the Apollo Theater in Harlem had gone well. Also, throughout the tour, the Motortown Revue had the impact Berry had hoped for, so he knew it was possible to leave the chitlin circuit behind. By December 1962, as the tour ended, Motown's performers had gained increased recognition. Record sales had grown. And Motown singers and musicians were now earning and retaining top dollar for their talent.

Most of them had never dreamed they'd make such large amounts of money or experience such stardom. During the tour, Berry had set up a system whereby the money performers earned was deposited directly into each of their personal bank accounts. Since many of the kids were still underage, Berry wanted to protect them from spending frivolously.

Berry was pleased with the success of the Motortown Revue, but like a car's engine on a winter morning, Motown was just warming up.

Child, it's like this. Each time Motown's success grew, Berry was eager to groom—and zoom—his company. And that's just what he did. He put a shine on his performers and sent them soaring.

MISS MANNERS

HEY, KID, LOOK OVER HERE.

You see the needle on our speedometer inching forward? Can you feel our wheels moving us ahead a little faster? That's exactly what Motown did. When the calendar turned to 1963, Hitsville rolled into high gear.

Berry already knew that Motown's music had broad appeal, and now it was time to push the company to greater heights. Berry had been taking notes when he traveled with the Motortown Revue, and it became clear to him that his performers sounded good, but they didn't have the right moves to deliver their songs with style.

While belting out the refrain of "Shop Around," Smokey Robinson and the Miracles would be off step, nearly bumping into one another, and wishing their mamas had told them how to dance and sing at the same time. And the Marvelettes needed "Mr. Postman" to deliver some suggestions on how to sway on cue!

Berry realized that recording vocals in a studio where nobody saw you wasn't the same as performing in a theater or nightclub in front of an audience. Live shows required stage presence, but many of the Motown performers were still rough around the edges.

One singer who showed great promise was Berry's brother-in-law Marvin Gaye, who was a background drummer at Motown. In addition to his talent on the drums, Marvin had gained singing experience in church. He was the son of a fiery preacher and had grown up learning that a man's voice could have great influence. Marvin sang in a way that inspired people.

Berry saw Marvin's potential to become a headliner. Marvin was handsome. Marvin was sexy. Marvin's voice was crushed velvet and caramel rolled into one.

But for all that smooth singing, Marvin was very shy and short on confidence. Whenever it was time to perform, he had more than butterflies in his stomach. He was plagued with big-winged bats who had a flapping party in Marvin's belly every time he was about to go onstage. As much as Marvin loved to sing, performances were painful for him. Whenever he sang, though, the ladies in the audience went wild for his soulful tenor-baritone voice. Berry took notice of this and made a commitment to help develop Marvin into a more self-assured entertainer.

Now Berry began to take steps to build a new Motown department called Artist Development, a division that would groom performers.

Berry believed Motown's talent was worthy of settings that packed more class than those along the chitlin circuit. He wanted to get his artists into places where black entertainers were not often allowed to perform, such as elegant theaters and swanky supper clubs in New York City and Las Vegas, where audiences

Marvin Gaye could croon a tune like nobody else. He started his Motown career as a successful balladeer.

consisted of mostly white patrons. On Berry's dream list of possible gigs were New York's Copacabana showroom and the Flamingo Hotel in Las Vegas.

Berry's aspirations didn't stop there. He was eager to see his performers appear on national television. An appearance on a TV program could catapult a singing group's career into overnight mega-stardom.

To get his singers ready for the mainstream, Berry purchased a building across the street from Hitsville U.S.A., where he set up Motown's Artist Development program. To expand Motown, he had purchased several houses in the neighborhood. These additional buildings would be used for dance studios, rehearsal spaces, and more offices.

Berry's sisters Anna and Gwen began to conduct classes for the performers on how to present themselves in public. In addition to running a photo concession booth, they had also once been fashion models. Right away, Anna and Gwen realized how unsophisticated the Motown singers were. Through their record sales, many of them had already become stars, but these stars needed some serious polishing to shine their brightest. Most of the singers had no idea how much grooming they required.

Berry's sisters persuaded their brother to hire their modeling instructor, Maxine Powell, to head up Motown's Artist Development program. Maxine had owned Detroit's first African American modeling agency and finishing school. She was a beautiful, smart, tough, straight-talking taskmaster who didn't put up with any back talk or bad attitudes. People called her Miss Manners.

When Miss Manners arrived at the house on West Grand Boulevard, she took charge immediately. She told the artists she was getting them ready for the White House and Buckingham Palace. She explained that if they wanted to become impressive enough to sing for royalty, they needed to go from crude to classy.

It was mandatory that every Motown singer attend Maxine's classes a few days a week. Right away, Marvin Gaye told Maxine that he didn't need charm school. Maxine corrected Marvin, telling him that her classes were not charm school—they were *finishing* school. What she taught was more than charm. She was giving lessons in elegance and etiquette that would serve him for life.

Marvin insisted that his life didn't need elegance or *finishing*. Well, Miss Manners told Marvin Gaye the honest-to-goodness truth about himself. He kept his eyes closed when he sang so that people thought he was asleep onstage. She

imitated how Marvin looked like a tired turtle when he slouched. She explained that her lessons would boost his confidence and make it easier to sing in front of an audience. This was enough convincing for Marvin.

Like Berry, Maxine had rules—the Stops and the Starts.

Stop snapping your gum.

Stop swivel-necking when you speak.

Stop slumping your shoulders.

Stop protruding your patootie when you walk.

Stop picking your teeth when you eat.

And for goodness' sake, *stop* cursing!

Maxine's Start list was even longer:

Start looking people in the eye when you greet them. (This was especially important for Marvin.)

Start reading the newspaper and books so that you can speak about current events and culture.

Start standing up straight.

Start tucking in your butt.

Start putting your napkin in your lap before you eat a meal.

Start lifting your chin.

Start conversations by smiling.

Marvin Gaye often looked pained when he sang. That's because he suffered from severe stage fright. Whenever Marvin performed, his nervousness was front and center until he got lessons in showmanship from Motown's etiquette instructor, Maxine Powell.

Maxine demonstrated how the girls were to stand with one foot slightly forward. How to push your hip bones outward when you cross from one side of a room to the other. How to properly pick up a hankie if you drop it. How to glide instead of walk. How, if your slip comes down around your ankles, to step out of it gracefully and keep on gliding.

Maxine showed the men, too. How to open a door for a lady. How to place a stole around a woman's shoulders. How to present your palm faced upward while helping a lady step out of a car.

Just as important as practicing rules of etiquette was dressing and grooming properly. Maxine spent hours selecting clothes for the performers, making sure the colors she chose complimented their complexions. It was Maxine's responsibility to develop the wardrobes of her students, while at the same time being mindful of Motown's clothing budget.

From her modeling days, Maxine knew how to dress like a millionaire without spending a fortune. She shopped at bridal stores and turned bridesmaid dresses into star-quality show clothes by sewing on rhinestones and sequins. For men, Maxine purchased secondhand tuxedos that she bedazzled with satin lapels and velvet elbow patches.

Personal hygiene was as important as clothes. Maxine insisted that young women always had their hair done and that hairdos were smooth.

This meant that on a Friday night, hair was fried, dyed, laid to the side, and wrapped in a scarf before saying good night. Under Maxine's tutelage, fingernails were polished in peach or tangerine. Eyebrows were plucked every week. Acceptable eye shadow colors were robin's egg blue or aquamarine. Feather duster eyelashes—the glue-on kind that flutter when you blink—made shy eyes shine.

Teeth had to be brushed three times a day. Frosted lipstick was blot, blot, blotted, so it wasn't blotchy.

Maxine Powell brought a touch of class to Motown's acts by teaching teens how to dress, speak, and behave like ladies and gentlemen. Shown here long after she'd served as the head of Hitsville's Artist Development department, the lady never lost her sense of style.

Men got manicured, too. Bye-bye dirt under the fingernails. Hello, cuticle cream, Murray's Pomade hair dressing, and Cherry Blossom shoe polish.

Maxine believed that teaching Motown performers the rules of proper conduct and dressing them in flashy threads meant more than just prettifying some kids off the street. Maxine was deeply committed to equality. She wanted to help Berry achieve his dream of crossover success. Once mainstream audiences got a look at her protégés, they would immediately see that true stars have no color. They just shine! Honey, Maxine Powell was a lady on a mission. To her, grooming the Motown singers was an important step in racial progress.

CHOLLY'S MOVES

FINISHING SCHOOL WAS NOT THE ONLY THING THE MOTOWN PERFORMERS NEEDED TO GET INTO CLASSY VENUES.

Berry had observed that if his performers wanted to make it in show business, they needed more than to *look* smooth—they needed to be able to move. They had to be able to get down with the groove. These kids needed rhythm, child. Dance skills. Something called *choreography*.

When Berry saw the sorry dance steps his performers were attempting to do during their tour, he started to ask around for someone who could help. In order to teach his singers how to bring their performances alive with flashy dancing, Berry added a choreography program to his Artist Development department. He hired Cholly Atkins as part of the Artist Development team. Cholly was a New York City choreographer who had been a member of the famous dance team Coles and Atkins.

Cholly Atkins worked with many Motown groups on bringing style to their moves. Acting out the words of a song was part of Cholly's technique. Here he shows the Four Tops how to put their best feet forward.

Cholly had performed as a dancer on Broadway and toured with musical greats Count Basie and Duke Ellington. He had worked with R&B groups who had appeared at Harlem's Apollo Theater. Like Maxine Powell, Cholly was keen on seeing Motown succeed. He shared Berry's vision of getting Motown acts into mainstream theaters as a means of breaking down racial barriers and the negative stereotypes about the abilities of black performers to impress white audiences.

Maxine had done such a good job teaching her pupils how to behave politely that they didn't complain or whine one bit when Cholly came to town. His first lesson was a dance technique he called "vocal choreography." This was a strategy vocalists used to breathe properly so that they could sing, two-step, spin, twist, and shimmy, all at the same time, while keeping their composure.

You see, kid, people think singing and dancing together is easy. But try it. It's hard not to run out of breath while belting your heart out and getting on the good foot. And it's even more difficult to do this with four of your friends, all trying to stay on the beat.

This was part of Cholly's challenge. He had to teach Motown's groups to move in a synchronized fashion. Each group needed something different depending on their size, music, and aptitude.

The Motown group called the Contours, they were some big dudes. Teaching them to dance was like instructing football players how to be light on their feet. Cholly showed the Contours how to go from clunky to suave by expressing their songs with hand motions, shoulder sways, and step-touch moves.

For the girl groups, it was important to convey grace, fluidity, and a touch of sex appeal that wasn't considered in poor taste.

One of Cholly's greatest strengths was creating choreography that, like the lyrics to many Motown songs, told a story. This involved acting.

Child, how many times have you stood in front of your mirror singing a love song with both hands over your heart?

And when you're crooning about love gone wrong, I know you can't help but pretend to be wiping the tears from your eyes. Or, when the lyrics turn to the part of the song about a happy sunrise, it's darn near impossible not to spread your arms wide, wiggle your fingers, and make believe you are Mother Sun coming up over a far horizon.

We have Cholly Atkins to thank for that. He defined the art of singing pantomime.

What? You never did anything like that?

Well, here are the steps to make it happen, Cholly-style:

1. Glide up to a full-length mirror.
2. Wave at yourself (after all, you *do* look good).
3. Pay yourself a compliment. Say, "Hey, you *fine* thing."
4. Sing these words and follow the moves:

I love my baby, yes I do (Place hands on heart.)

But my baby's found someone new (Look surprised.)

To tell the truth, it makes me blue (Make like you're crying and wiping your eyes.)

When my baby's new love did my baby wrong (Fold your arms, turn your back to the mirror.)

Came cryin' to me, singing a whole new song (Pretend you're pleading.)

Took my baby back on one condition (Wag a finger at your baby.)

Our love would now have a new rendition (Hand on hip.)

Yes, our love would now have a new rendition (Both hands on hips. Nod once, like you really mean it.)

How did that feel?

Good, right?

Yeah, I *know.*

When Cholly taught these kinds of steps to Smokey, Marvin, Mary, the Contours, and other Motown singers, they were also enthused to move. We can applaud Cholly Atkins for bringing the smooth to Motown's performers—and to you.

DANCING IN THE STREET

SWEETIE, THIS IS THE PART OF OUR RHYTHM RIDE THAT HUGS THE ROAD.

Along here, the pavement hums. We're heading into Motown's golden time. As 1963 approached, Hitsville U.S.A. was definitely living up to its name. Marvin Gaye recorded a song called "Hitch Hike," which became a Top 40 hit and took him from a background drummer to a front-and-center star.

"Hitch Hike" kicked off a string of successes for Marvin. He recorded "Pride and Joy" and "Can I Get a Witness," which also became hits.

Thanks to Maxine's finishing school, Marvin no longer slouched. Though he still sometimes closed his eyes when he sang, it was because he was moved by the emotions his songs conveyed, not because he was nervous. From that point on, everybody who sang Marvin's songs did it just like Marvin, with eyes closed when hitting the high notes. That's the power of music that touches your soul. It rouses you, child. Stirs you from the inside out.

Martha Reeves and the Vandellas started out by singing at church benefits and YMCA parties. They originally called themselves the Del Phis and the Vels before changing their name. The girls blew the roof off the record charts.

Martha Reeves also went from a Motown hopeful to a hit-maker. She and her group, the Vandellas, had been singing backup vocals for Marvin Gaye.

Then one day, luck smiled on Martha and her two friends. Mary Wells had been scheduled to sing in a recording session for a song called "(Love Is Like a) Heat Wave." But Mary wasn't there at the start time. On this particular day, she was late, and nobody could seem to reach her.

The musicians waited and waited for Mary.

Berry waited and waited for Mary.

More than anybody, Martha Reeves *really* waited for Mary. She was secretly hoping that Mary would not show up and that she'd be able to fill in.

Finally, when it was determined that Mary would be absent that day, Martha jumped at the opportunity. She stepped in, coming on strong with her powerful gospel voice. Martha was only twenty-two years old, but her vocals packed the wisdom of someone with many years of singing experience.

In just a few short months, Martha and the Vandellas had two hit songs in the Top 10. "(Love Is Like a) Heat Wave" was a breakthrough hit that peaked at number four on the *Billboard* magazine Hot 100 list, and at number one on the *Billboard* R&B Singles Chart.

The Vandellas' next hit, "Quicksand," became another Top 10, rising to number eight on the *Billboard* Hot 100 chart.

With her newly established fame, Martha kissed her receptionist desk a fast goodbye. She slipped into a classy satin dress that had a flower-petal peplum (purchased by Maxine, of course), and Martha *sang*.

Kid, let's turn on our car radio and listen to "(Love Is Like a) Heat Wave" right now. You hear that gospel backbeat and those jazz overtones? They make you wanna get up out of your seat, don't they? The Vandellas' soul-siren vocals are what set them apart from other Motown groups.

"(Love Is Like a) Heat Wave" is the perfect song for working some Cholly Atkins dance magic. And the lyrics employ Motown's songs-that-tell-a-story concept that Berry Gordy understood so well.

In "Heat Wave," as the song came to be called, Martha sings about a guy who has her heart "burning with desire."

To make matters even hotter, the song's narrator tells everybody she's "going insane" over her feelings of love.

Then the song puts it to us by asking, "Is this the way love's supposed to be?"

One of the best parts of "Heat Wave" is its doo-wop call-and-response vocals. That's what makes the song fun to sing with your friends.

As for choreography, it's simple. Just fan yourself, and your heat waving will be so hot it'll be cool.

If you've ever endured a real heat wave, you know that putting up with a sweaty neck and sticky armpits is no picnic. In Detroit during the summer the days can be stifling. But when you're a Motown songwriter, nothing stifles creativity.

Collaboration was the name of the game for brothers Brian and Eddie Holland and their friend Lamont Dozier. They were a songwriting team that became a hit-making machine. Known as H-D-H, the trio wrote chart toppers for countless Motown artists. The songs they created often came from their own personal experiences. A memorable date with a girl or fun times at a party sometimes turned up in a tune set to catchy lyrics.

This was especially true for Brian and Eddie Holland, who had been Berry's friends ever since they were all kids back in school. The two brothers were ace storytellers. They had a special talent for writing poems and for spinning words together in ways that made you remember them. That's what lyrics of the best songs are, child. They're poems set to a melody that tell a story.

The songs that become hits—the ones we all sing and sing and sing—are made up of melody poems that stick.

Brian and Eddie joined together with their friend Lamont Dozier and formed a songwriting team called Holland-Dozier-Holland or, as they came to be known in the neighborhood, H-D-H.

Through their lyrics, H-D-H spun music-beauty that made vinyl records glisten.

Having grown up in the Motor City, Brian, Eddie, and Lamont understood how, as in a factory, they could mass-produce songs and also keep the wheels of their creativity greased.

H-D-H never sat back in cruise control.

When the sun rose, they *wrote*. When the lunch bell rang, they crafted lyrics that had a ring to them.

Have you ever eaten dinner while sitting at the piano plunking out a poem? That's how H-D-H spent most of their days.

Late nights were the same. For this amazing team, the *wee* hours became the *we* hours, when they worked together to create songs that would end up as hits. Sometimes H-D-H could finish three songs in one day's time.

The group would often start with Eddie's verse. Then Brian would come up with the music. Lamont was a lyricist *and* a musician.

One of H-D-H's early successes was "(Love Is Like a) Heat Wave." That song was just the beginning of what would be a string of hits.

H-D-H was a team of pros whose names seldom appeared in the spotlight, but whose brilliance made the spotlight possible for many Motown stars.

William "Mickey" Stevenson and Ivy Jo Hunter were another team of songwriters who loomed large at Motown. Like H-D-H, they were a quiet force not known to many people by their names.

Mickey was the head of Motown's Artist & Repertoire department, known as "A&R" by people in the music business. He was an important member of the Motown family whose impact was felt as Motown was really starting to take off.

It was Mickey's job to match the right songs with the groups or soloists who could perform them in the best ways. Mickey was also responsible for developing ideas, writing songs, and producing them.

When summer poured its heat onto the streets of Detroit, Mickey noticed that kids liked to cool off by playing in the water that gushed from open fire hydrants. To Mickey, it looked like the kids were dancing in the water. The way they hopped and dodged on the pavement was like a splashy bash. This inspired Mickey. He conceived of a song about a summer street party where everybody's out in the streets dancing. Mickey got in touch with his songwriter friend, Ivy Jo.

Child, you know how people like to kick back in the summertime, drink lemonade, and wait for a breeze? Mickey and Ivy weren't like that at all. Summer's hot-as-heck temperatures lit a fuse under their ingenuity.

Ivy Jo and Mickey crafted lyrics to a song about the familiar scene of kids splashing in fire hydrant water and showed the words of their song to their buddy Marvin Gaye. Even though the song was inspired by kids playing, Ivy Jo and

Mickey thought it might pack more soul as a slow ballad. Marvin told his friends the song was meant for dancing, not swooning, and he helped them rework the song's composition.

One day, Martha Reeves heard the songwriters tinkering and asked if she could arrange the song to fit her vocals and those of the Vandellas.

They all agreed and went into Hitsville's recording studio to see what Martha and the Vandellas could do. Honey, they did it right. Those ladies nabbed it in two takes. The song's musicians brought it even more alive with a clanging backbeat that was made by rattling tire chains, and "Dancing in the Street," as we know it today, was born.

"Dancing in the Street" is more than a song. It's a feel-good celebration. The song's premise is that in any city, anywhere, dancing and partying in the hot summer streets is fun.

"Dancing in the Street" was released in July 1964. As soon as that record *hit* the streets, its dancing peaked at number two on the *Billboard* magazine Pop Singles chart.

As soon as every kitty cat, chickadee, alley rat, and kid heard Martha's brassy vocals, they knew that summer's heat was a blessing.

Whether they lived in Detroit, Chicago, New York City, New Orleans, Philadelphia, Baltimore, or D.C., they had an invitation to this party, where the dance floor was the pavement.

"Dancing in the Street" went on to be one of Motown's signature singles, and Martha and the Vandellas' most famous song.

People referred to it as a dance anthem.

For me, kid, "Dancing in the Street" is a praise song and a hallelujah hymn, rolled into one unforgettable party starter.

WONDER KID

MARTHA REEVES'S SUCCESS SHOWED HOW A SINGER COULD HANG AROUND MOTOWN AND BE DISCOVERED.

If Berry Gordy saw something special in a youngster, he would sign him or her to a Motown record deal.

One morning, Berry was enjoying breakfast in his office when Mickey Stevenson rushed in, excited to speak to him. Most folks don't like having their bacon and eggs interrupted, but Mickey urged Berry to stop eating. Ronnie White, a member of the Miracles, had invited a ten-year-old boy to come to Hitsville U.S.A. Mickey told Berry he *had* to come to the recording studio to hear this child sing.

Before Berry even got to the studio, he heard the boy pounding his bongo drums and playing his harmonica. When Berry stepped into the room, he was surprised to find that the kid musician, Steveland Morris, was completely blind.

He had a sharp, pitchy little-kid voice that warbled when he hit a high C, but Berry saw something in him right away. Steveland had a keen ability to listen to music, singing, and the inflections in people's speaking voices, and to imitate these perfectly.

Steveland had taught himself to play instruments and to sing by spending hours listening to the radio. Also, this kid was quick. He learned musical concepts easily and put them into practice. He could bounce from one instrument to another, becoming a master at each one. Berry invited Steveland to observe the Motown family by encouraging him to spend time at 2648 West Grand Boulevard, taking pointers from the other musicians.

Steveland had a natural poise. Though he was sent to Maxine Powell's finishing school, Miss Manners had very little work to do on Steveland's showmanship. He seemed to already know what it took.

The more time Steveland spent in the Motown building, the more accomplished he became at playing the drums, harmonica, piano, and bass, and at improving his vocal ability. Steveland was soon able to modify his warbly singing voice so that instead of a high-pitched shrill, it was a beautiful ribbon of sound.

Berry Gordy couldn't believe his eyes when he met Steveland Morris for the first time. He was surprised to see that this talented musician was a blind kid who could bring bongo drum beats alive.

Berry once remarked that this boy was a wonder. From that day on, everybody called him by the nickname Little Stevie Wonder.

When Stevie was eleven years old, Berry offered him a contract with Motown. That was back in 1961. It was the beginning of this kid wonder achieving greatness.

Because Stevie was a minor, strict child-labor laws allowed him to work only a certain number of hours each day and restricted his travel. Adding to this was Little Stevie's stern mother, Lula Hardaway.

Lula loved her boy. She was always looking out for her son's well-being.

Lula insisted that Berry provide a tutor for Stevie.

That Stevie always travel with a record producer.

That Stevie get in bed early.

That Stevie eat right.

That Stevie have enough time to relax between gigs.

That Stevie, Stevie, Stevie be treated like a true professional.

Berry didn't like having so many Stevie rules put to him, but he respected Lula's wishes and understood that this child's mother was doing what any mother would do if her fifth grader was working his way toward stardom.

Stevie was a jokester. With his sense of humor, he made fast friends among the people at Motown. Stevie became a great impersonator of Berry Gordy. Sometimes he'd call people up on the telephone and, pretending to be Berry, would insist that someone get a new tape recorder for that cute boy Stevie Wonder.

In the spring of 1963, when Motown was cruising smoothly on the road to success, Little Stevie hit it big by mistake. It happened when the recording of a song called "Fingertips Part 2" was released as a two-part single.

The year before, in June 1962, Stevie had been performing with several Motown acts in a live show at the Regal Theater in Chicago. The performance was being recorded.

Stevie played "Fingertips," a mostly instrumental piece that showcased his wizardry on the bongo drums and harmonica. The audience went wild, deep-diggin' Stevie's music.

As "Fingertips" was finishing, Stevie belted to the audience, "Everybody say yeah!"

And, yeah, everybody was on-point with Stevie.

This sparked an "everybody say yeah" call and response between Little Stevie Wonder and every ticket holder in the place. You could hear the yeahs from the front-row premium seats all the way to the theater's nosebleed section.

Stevie showed his appreciation by putting so much breath into his harmonica solo that the silver on that instrument seemed to have wings. The audience's clapping was full of hard, good rhythm.

To add to the fun, Stevie tossed the melody from "Mary Had a Little Lamb" into the mix. I know that if Mary had been in the audience that night, her little lamb would have been jamming big-time with Little Stevie.

Thinking he'd taken "Fingertips" as far as he could, Stevie started to make his exit off the stage.

But the crowd was still hyped up!

They wanted *more*.

They wanted an *encore*.

They wanted to keep pouring their praises onto Little Stevie Wonder. The band began to play their exit music. But this was far from goodbye.

Stevie got so swept up in the moment that he bounced back into action. Stevie's bass player had left the stage, but Mary Wells's bassist, Larry Moses, was setting up for the next number, a song to be sung by Mary.

Larry couldn't ignore the screaming audience. And there was no way to deny Stevie's enthusiasm. It didn't take much to see that this kid's luster was just lighting up. He called out to Stevie, "What key? What key?"

When Larry hit the C minor that was the key to the "Fingertips" frenzy, the raw spontaneity sparked "Fingertips Part 2," which came on quick, like an unexpected burst of fun. Stevie lifted his harmonica to his lips and pumped that instrument with a soul-blowing solo that was accompanied by the audience clapping to his rhythm.

By August 1963, American teenagers were reaching *their* fingertips deep into their wallets to purchase the "Fingertips"/ "Fingertips Part 2" single. The record's A-side was the live version of "Fingertips." The "Fingertips Part 2" encore was the record's B-side. It became the number one hit on the *Billboard* magazine Pop and R&B Singles charts. And, it was Motown's second number one pop hit after the Marvelettes' "Please Mr. Postman."

"Fingertips Part 2" was magic for Stevie. It was his first Motown recording, and it catapulted his career as the singer on a single record and on an album titled *Recorded Live: The 12 Year Old Genius*, which was a collection of Stevie's songs released at the same time as the "Fingertips" single.

Recorded Live: The 12 Year Old Genius reached number one on the *Billboard* magazine Pop Albums chart. Stevie was the youngest artist to ever accomplish this.

That's pretty remarkable, kid, isn't it? The name Wonder fit Stevie like a glove whose fingertips were custom-made for his incredible talent.

"Fingertips" is one of those songs that make audiences go wild with excitement. Whenever Stevie performed the hit, and told everybody to "Say yeah," they did more than say it—they shouted, shook, and snapped to his finger-tipping beats.

THE FUNK BROTHERS

BY 1964, THE POP MUSIC CHARTS MIGHT AS WELL HAVE BEEN CALLED THE MOTOWN MUSIC CHARTS, 'CAUSE SONGS THAT WERE SUNG BY HITSVILLE'S PERFORMERS WERE ALL OVER THEM.

The Miracles, who dominated the charts, were sure living up to their name. Given that they'd started out as regular kids from the streets of Detroit, their success *had* been miraculous. The same was true of chart-toppers Marvin Gaye, Martha and the Vandellas, the Marvelettes, the Contours, and Little Stevie Wonder (whose popularity was now far from little).

These performers were leading the Motown hit parade. But let me introduce you to some folks whose names weren't in the spotlight. Like many of the Motown songwriters, these were people whose contributions to the success of Hitsville's songs were just as important as the ones who did the crooning.

These guys were what people call behind-the-scenes folks. Not many fans saw them, but everybody who loved a Motown hit loved what these dudes did.

Speaking as the Groove, I know what it's like to be in the background. Nobody ever *sees* me. But they *feel* me, child. Yes, they *feel* me.

Because of me, they keep the beat. That's why behind the scenes is a beautiful place to be. Without it, there'd be no strength in front and center. You see, child, there's backbone in the background.

In the same way that Berry scouted for singers at Detroit high schools, he also hung out in jazz clubs, on the lookout for talented backup musicians.

During the many years that the Funk Brothers played behind Motown's singers at recording sessions, the group's members changed. But their unforgettable music always brought the funk. Left to right, Hank Crosby, Larry Veeder, Joe Hunter, James Jamerson, Mike Terry, and Benny Benjamin.

One night, very early in Motown's history, Berry visited a Detroit nightspot that was wide awake and *jamming*. It was deep into the darkest hours, when the clock had already struck twelve, then one o'clock, and was inching its way to two in the morning, and the Funk Brothers, a hot backup band, had brought the beat to every corner of the place. Drummer Benny "Papa Zita" Benjamin, bassist James Jamerson, guitarist Robert White, keyboardist Earl Van Dyke, and band-leader Joe Hunter had turned the night sizzling bright. A few days later, Berry brought these musicians into the Motown studios. He gave each of them a long-term contract and made them important members of the Hitsville family. Additional Funk Brothers band members included Hank Crosby, Larry Veeder, and Mike Terry. Other Funk Brothers were Clarence Isabell, who played the double bass; Richard "Pistol" Allen, a drummer; Paul Riser, an ace on the trombone; and guitarists Eddie Willis and Joe Messina. And Jack Ashford, Jack Brokensha, and Eddie "Bongo" Brown put a capital *F* in *Funk* as they flawlessly played the tambourine, vibraphone, marimba, and a host of other instruments.

In time, keyboardist Johnny Griffith became a Funk Brother, along with Uriel Jones, who joined the band as a third drummer. Bassist Bob Babbitt and guitarist Dennis Coffey were also among the funkiest brothers in town.

These musicians had talent and imagination. Who says backup music can be played with only traditional instruments? They used whatever it took to bring their sound alive. This included banging wood blocks together, jangling chains, creating a chorus of clapping hands, and stomping their heels.

From Motown's beginnings, the Funk Brothers played backup on most of Hitsville's recordings.

While enjoying Motown music, millions of kids were also listening, dancing, bopping, snapping, and singing praises to the Funk Brothers' brilliance, without even knowing it.

The Funk Brothers seldom traveled for live performances. Berry kept them as an in-house band so they would always be available for late-night recording sessions.

You might think it's not fair that these great musicians didn't get much public recognition. Heck, there's even a movie about them called *Standing in the Shadows of Motown*.

But if you *really* think about it, a shadow is long and large, and it makes an undeniable impression.

UGLY SIGHTSEEING

NOW, KID, WE COME TO A PART OF THE RHYTHM RIDE THAT'S NOT ALL HARMONICAS AND BONGOS.

Every trip you make will take you to places that aren't so scenic. Every road has potholes.

But we have to stay on course, child. The only way forward is *through*. So tighten your seat belt, 'cause I need to show you this part of the highway. I have to.

You see that exit sign ahead?

It's the one that says "Road Under Construction—Beware of Danger."

Well, we're turning off here for a moment, so I can show you why Motown was so important, and how it changed the road as we know it.

With the success of Smokey Robinson and the Miracles, Mary Wells, Marvin Gaye, Martha Reeves and the Vandellas, and Stevie Wonder, Motown had achieved great things.

With Hitsville U.S.A.'s offices dominating West Grand Boulevard, Detroit had gone from being called "The Motor City" to "The Music City."

Berry had accomplished the goals he'd set for building a profitable music recording and publishing company.

Motown singers, songwriters, and producers were finally earning good money for their work and receiving the royalty income they deserved.

Motown music was immediately recognizable. The sing-along lyrics, gospel-inspired rhythms, and bubblegum-soul harmonies had come to be called "The Motown Sound."

Part of this special sound—the reverberation of tones—happened in Hitsville's "echo chamber," a small room in the house with a hole in the ceiling that opened into the attic. Berry had figured out that music could be piped up through the hole, then recorded to capture an echoing sound. This made the music swell, so it gave off its own special roundness.

And, kid, here's an insider tone tip from the Groove. You can get a similar sound by singing in the shower, without cutting a hole through any ceilings.

In many respects, Motown's Rhythm Ride was going along very smoothly. Hitsville U.S.A. was redefining music.

But as Motown's triumphs were picking up speed, America was entering one of the most turbulent times in its history.

Look, child.

Check out the scene as we drive back in time.

Do you see it?

There it is. In the rearview mirror.

It's easy to fall asleep on long rides, especially as we enter a dark part of this trip.

But please pay close attention. Especially now, as I explain what you're looking at.

I'm gonna slow our roll just a bit so you don't miss anything.

I need to warn you. This is scary. You are about to witness things that have made grown people cry.

See those African Americans? Those proud, beautiful men and women?

They had grown weary of the discrimination they'd endured under the Jim Crow segregation laws, which prevented them from having the same privileges as white citizens.

Most African Americans still earned less money than white people, and they were kept from gaining equal pay or opportunities for job advancement.

Although laws had been passed that prevented segregation in public schools, in many states, black students and white students still attended separate schools. Black students still had shabby books, broken pencils, and rickety desks.

If Little Stevie Wonder had entered sixth grade at Miller Middle School in Detroit, he would have had to put up with inferior materials and conditions.

Look at all those children trying to make sense of their tattered books. See that little boy crying? He wants to learn about planets and mountains and clouds. But how can he learn when his textbooks are missing so many pages?

His parents want to make a change, but back then African Americans were still prevented from fair voting in elections.

In parts of the South, if you were African American and wanted a burger and a Coke at a lunch counter, you would not be served at a "Whites Only" restaurant. And, chances are, if you were African American, some prejudiced person would try to get rid of you by spitting in your face or pouring hot coffee over your head.

Spit on your lip or in your french fries doesn't taste good. And it hurts to get scalded with coffee when all you want to do is have a good meal.

There were worse things, too. Black people were the victims of hate crimes such as lynchings and bomb raids. Kids your same age suffered ugly violence.

On March 2, 1955, a teenager named Claudette Colvin refused to give up her seat on a bus in Montgomery, Alabama, to a white woman after the driver demanded it. Claudette was dragged off the bus backward while being kicked by police and handcuffed on her way to the police station.

Just a few months later in Money, Mississippi, on August 28, 1955, a fourteen-year-old boy named Emmett Till was beaten and shot to death because he supposedly whistled at a white woman in a grocery store. His dead, bloated body was found days later by two boys fishing in the Tallahatchie River.

Emmett Till was tortured and killed by white men after it was reported that he'd whistled at a white woman. He was a kid from Chicago who was on his summer vacation in Mississippi. Here, he's shown with his mom before he left for his trip down South. He never made it home.

On September 15, 1963, in Birmingham, Alabama, four friends—Carole Robertson, Cynthia Wesley, Denise McNair, and Addie Mae Collins—went to church, ready to pray.

They were killed by a man with a bomb, who had tucked his hatred under the steps of that church and run away before the bomb's blast took the lives of those little girls.

Carol Denise McNair, Carole Robertson, Addie Mae Collins, and Cynthia Wesley were victims of a terrorist act when their church, the 16th Street Baptist Church, was bombed by members of the Ku Klux Klan. The girls didn't get out alive.

It's unthinkable.

But it's all true.

Sweetheart, I know this part of the journey is painful.

Lord knows, I let the tears flow every time I pass this way. Even the Groove gets the blues.

These tragic events made Berry very sad, too. He wanted to help change the evil that was prejudice against African American people. He looked for ways to make things better.

Berry Gordy wasn't the only one with hope in his heart. Civil rights leader Martin Luther King, Jr., also had a dream of equality, which he shared on August 28, 1963, with 250,000 people at the March on Washington for Jobs and Freedom, in Washington, D.C.

Martin told the world about his hope that someday all of us could work together. Pray together. Stand up for freedom together.

Martin's "I Have a Dream" speech inspired many people. It especially resonated with Berry, who in August 1963 released an album that included an earlier version of the speech that Martin had delivered at a freedom rally in Detroit on June 23, 1963.

That album was called *The Great March to Freedom*. It featured Martin's speech as well as speeches by other notable civil rights leaders.

The Great March to Freedom was the first and only record of its kind. It preserved one of the most memorable speeches ever delivered, and it showed the world that Motown wasn't just making music. Hitsville U.S.A. was making history, taking the high road, and helping to move the fight for justice forward.

So let's keep driving, child. There's hope up ahead.

SUNSHINE ON A CLOUDY DAY

Look, there's a slice of bright coming through the clouds.

As America slowly marched in its struggle to become a nation of equality, Motown's music continued to glisten.

Think about it, kid. When stars twinkle in the sky, all kinds of people can enjoy their sparkling beauty. When the sun rises, its light shines on everyone. When the moon is full and spilling its milk, the white hope of its glow inspires every soul.

These same qualities were true of Motown's songs. Their radiance brought enormous joy.

Berry believed that all people share the same emotions, no matter where they live, what color they are, what language they speak, or which religion they choose to follow. He also knew that music has the power to express these emotions and to foster harmony among people. He said, "Communication breeds understanding, and understanding breeds everything else." Berry recognized that music is a language everybody can comprehend.

At the end of 1963, Berry devised a plan to make Motown's music accessible to even more people. He structured a deal with EMI, a record company that would sell Motown's songs internationally. This way, teens overseas could experience the Motown sound.

If a girl or boy in some far-off land wanted to purchase the Marvelettes' record before waiting by the mailbox to sing "Please Mr. Postman," they'd now be able to do it with ease. Or they could feel the sound right down to their own fingertips as they clapped their hands loud and proud to Little Stevie Wonder's *The 12 Year Old Genius*.

Once Berry's EMI distribution deal was finalized, love could be like a heat wave in London, Tokyo, Paris, and other places where "Whites Only" was a foreign concept.

The Four Tops sang R&B, soul, doo-wop, and jazz. Baritone Levi Stubbs, left, was their lead singer. Most male singing groups had a tenor out front, but Levi's deep voice made him worthy of the spotlight. Left to right, Obie Benson, Duke Fakir, and Lawrence Payton backed up Levi with their vocal power.

Even though Motown's music was starting to find an audience outside the United States, Berry continued to look for talent in his own hometown. And he continued to be very strategic about building the Motown roster.

Detroit's street corners and hangout joints swarmed with singers who now wanted to be affiliated with Motown. But not every singer was right for Hitsville U.S.A. When Berry met a vocalist or singing group, one of the first things he looked for was their ability to fit into the Motown family's code of ethics. If they were hardworking, honest, unselfish, humble, and eager to learn, Berry would consider signing them up at Motown. A performer could have a tremendous voice or stage presence, but if he or she was greedy, self-centered, or puffed-up with a big ego, they could forget ever working at Hitsville U.S.A.

Obie Benson, Abdul "Duke" Fakir, Lawrence Payton, and Levi Stubbs had been buddies with Berry since childhood. They'd all grown up in the same Detroit neighborhood. These men weren't afraid of hard work. They'd come from strong, churchgoing families, so they knew what it meant to be among people who shared ideas, took an interest in others, and wanted the best for the group. Though they weren't related, Obie, Duke, Lawrence, and Levi were like brothers. They were a quartet who called themselves the Four Tops. Levi was their lead singer, whose *oooh-baby* baritone voice set the Four Tops apart from others.

Berry introduced H-D-H to the Four Tops. The pairing was better than a match made in heaven—it was a match made at Motown. The Four Tops became one of H-D-H's great inspirations. As soon as Brian, Eddie, and Lamont heard the Four Tops' raspy harmonizing, they wrote and wrote and wrote.

And oh, how the hit singles flowed!

In 1964, H-D-H created a musical piece called "Baby I Need Your Loving." At first, the song was purely instrumental. They looked for ways to bring the music alive. After many crack-of-dawn and late-night sessions, they added lyrics that speak to anyone who's ever loved anything or anybody.

The song's refrain—"Baby, I *neeeed* your lovin'"— is a plea that makes you want to get down on your knees, fold your hands, and beg for what's good.

In the two years that followed "Baby I Need Your Loving," H-D-H and the Four Tops made more beautiful music together. A song called "I Can't Help Myself (Sugar Pie Honey Bunch)" and one called "Reach Out I'll Be There" came next. They are, to this day, two of the most notable H-D-H and Four Tops songs. Both became *Billboard* magazine Hot 100 number one hits by flying up the chart faster than a mama robin flies to the top of a tree to take worms to her sugar-pie-honey-bunch babies in their nest. Seems everybody and *their* mamas loved those songs.

Obie, Duke, Lawrence, and Levi had experience performing in jazz clubs before they went to Motown and before they collaborated with H-D-H, but Berry insisted that they work with dance instructor Cholly Atkins. He wanted to be sure these Four Tops could stay at the top of their game.

Another group of male singers, called the Temptations, had come to Motown in 1961, before the Four Tops, but couldn't seem to capture the same thrill with their songs.

There were five Temptations, all in their early twenties. Elbridge "Al" Bryant, Melvin Franklin, Eddie Kendricks, Otis Williams, and Paul Williams had grown up together singing in church when they were boys.

All you had to do was look at these guys who were nicknamed the "Temptin' Temps" to see why they *were* so tempting. They were handsome, brown-skinned, and suave.

Cholly taught the Temptations all the right moves. They had a natural talent for choreography, but like all of Motown's performers, they still worked hard during rehearsals. Sometimes they would glisten with sweat after a full day of learning and practicing Cholly's choreography.

The Temptations could spin on cue, slide, glide, hip-swivel, and shuffle-step. Onstage, they were smoother than butter on warm waffles.

The Temptations (left to right), David Ruffin, Melvin Franklin, Paul Williams, Otis Williams, and Eddie Kendricks, originally called themselves The Elgins, but soon discovered that to win fans they needed a name that had more teen appeal. The quintet was known for its harmonies and flashy clothes.

Maxine Powell dressed them in velvet-lapel tuxedos, bow ties, and starched shirts. They looked as good as any of the other Motown performers, but their wardrobe took them only so far.

Berry tried to pair the Temptations with different songwriters, but nothing seemed to work. Even H-D-H couldn't land a winner for the Temptations.

Women swooned over their moves but not so much over their songs. Their on-point steps and soulful singing couldn't bring in a hit. The Temptations were tempting, but their songs were take-'em-or-leave-'em.

Berry believed in the Temptations. He knew they had what it took to be superstars. After years of trying to find a breakout tune for the Temptations, Berry finally came up with an idea. He announced a Motown family contest. The person who could write a hit song for the Temptations would be named the winner. Berry would even enter the contest himself.

Smokey Robinson was ready for the challenge. He already had a song in mind. It was a song he and fellow Miracles group member Bobby Rogers had begun when they were on the road as part of the Motortown Revue. Smokey and Bobby had considered the song a bit of a joke that they used to pass the time on the tour bus ride.

Soon after the contest was announced, Smokey and Bobby took out a pencil and some sheets of paper and started to play with the lyrics and melody they'd made up during their tour. Now, a year later, at the end of 1963, they realized that if they developed the lyrics and melody, they could make a possible hit for the Temptations.

The song started with something that makes everybody happy when they think about it—a smile so bright. Then they crafted the song around lyrics that used metaphors for everyday objects.

Once Smokey and Bobby put an image of a smile in people's minds, their song told listeners that if your smile lights up, you could be a *candle*. And if that smile makes me hug you, and hold you tight, then, baby, you could be a *handle*.

The name of their song was "The Way You Do the Things You Do." It was a tune that showed how Smokey Robinson, this time with the help of Bobby Rogers, did what *he* did with so much finesse that it was brighter than a carload of candles. The song was another example of Smokey Robinson's unique ability to make musical poetry that had wide appeal.

When "The Way You Do the Things You Do" shot to number eleven on the Top 40 hits chart, Smokey won the contest. Thanks to Smokey and Bobby, the Temptations went from a group of five guys who were *trying* to score a hit, to a quintet that had climbed out of the no-hit hole.

In 1964, just months after "The Way You Do the Things You Do" was released, David Ruffin replaced Al Bryant and became the sexy lead singer of the Temptations. Though the group had been at Motown for a few years and now had a hit single, David's arrival would take the quintet to even greater heights.

David had a voice that was spicy ginger and cream—it was gritty *and* mellow.

And he had thick glasses and hair that made him a pretty boy heartthrob in the eyes of the ladies. If you stopped a girl on the street and asked, "Which is your favorite Temp?" she was likely to say, "David Ruffin, the deep-chocolate one with those dreamy glasses."

With David as the lead singer and with Smokey's songwriting, the Temptations kept hitting it big. Smokey wrote and produced several songs that became classics. One of them is my all-time favorite Motown hit, a song called "My Girl."

When you're the Groove, some songs sink deep into every crevice of your being and live there forever. "My Girl" is one of those songs. It was the Temptations' first number one single. Since its release in 1964, it has sold millions of copies.

The song's lyrics and melody are for all those who have ever looked at the sky on a cloudy day, thought about their favorite girl, and, all of a sudden, noticed sunshine coming through the gloom.

"My Girl" is about walking down the street on a cold winter night, but feeling like the month of May is inside your socks because *your girl* is right there with you.

Child, you can sing "My Girl" to your sister, your mama, your best friend, your puppy, your granny, your favorite teacher, or the babysitter who lets you stay up late.

"My Girl" is one of Motown's most loved songs, mostly because it's *about* love. And even though it's been crooned by all kinds of people, the truth is, nobody has ever sung or performed "My Girl" like the Temptations. And nobody ever will.

Ever.

But hey, don't take my word for it. Listen for yourself.

Before David Ruffin became the lead singer for the Temptations, he worked as a contractor who did construction on the Hitsville U.S.A. building. His raspy singing voice caught the attention of Temptations group member Otis Williams, who invited David to join the group.

THE SOUND OF YOUNG AMERICA

THIS IS ONE MY FAVORITE PARTS OF MOTOWN'S RHYTHM RIDE.

We, kid, are on the *free*way. This is a moment in Motown's history when the view is beautiful everywhere you look. When we move into the fast lane and *soar*. This is where hit songs flew out from 2648 West Grand Boulevard like a flock of high-flying birds.

Smokey was on a hit-making roll with the Temptations, who proved themselves as a group that could deliver love songs with class.

But as their popularity grew—and with Motown's success from Martha and the Vandellas' "Dancing in the Street"—teens were eager to find even more records they could dance to. They also wanted to show the world they could turn on a party with their moves. Around this time, a dance craze called the Duck dominated the teen scene.

Facing page: Martha and the Vandellas gave new meaning to girl group dazzle. Though "Dancing in the Street" was a party song, many also considered its lyrics a celebration of African Americans showing their pride and solidarity as they gathered in their neighborhoods on summer evenings.

Child, you should have seen that dance. You would think a dance called the Duck starts and ends with a waddle. But honey, *this* duck had slick footwork and a backside that wouldn't quit. The Duck made even the shiest kids in town get up and shake some tail feathers. It was a dance that gave Smokey an idea for a Temptations song called "Get Ready."

Thanks to Norman Whitfield's know-how for bringing out the best from Motown's singers, the Temptations had just the right vocal blend when they recorded "Ain't Too Proud to Beg" under Whitfield's supervision.

With the Funk Brothers' Benny Benjamin slamming an up-tempo on his drum, "Get Ready" put an *uh-huh* to the Duck. The song became another bestseller on the Temptations hit list.

It was as if Smokey had waved an enchanted wand over the group and gave them a special ability to entertain in ways they hadn't been able to before.

While the Temptations were making their mark with the songs Smokey had written, a young songwriter named Norman Whitfield had been hanging out in the Motown control room watching and hoping for a chance to write a song.

Norman was one of those kids who was just always around. He was a quiet observer, learning all he could by listening and paying close attention. He'd been raised in Harlem but had come to Detroit in search of an opportunity to work at Hitsville U.S.A.

Norman never bothered anyone, but goodness, was he ever persistent. He would not go away. For him, spending day after day at Motown was like being in a special school. He *studied* the music, lyrics, and dance moves that were all around him.

Finally, someone at Motown hired Norman to work in the quality-control department. During the Friday morning meetings, he gave his honest-to-goodness opinion about songs that were being considered for release. He took what he'd learned and, one day, went off on his own and wrote a song for the Temptations called "Ain't Too Proud to Beg."

With "Ain't Too Proud to Beg," Norman nailed it.

As soon as that song was released in 1966, it shot to number thirteen on the *Billboard* pop music charts and was a number one hit on the *Billboard* R&B charts.

People everywhere put their pride in a back pocket, and no matter how silly they looked—with their faces all scrunched up pleading with the man at the record store who had just sold the last copy of the Temptations single—they begged and *begged* for that record.

Norman went on to write many popular songs for the Temptations, which were included, along with songs written by Smokey Robinson, on an album called *Greatest Hits (the Temptations Album)*. The album peaked at number five on *Billboard*'s Top Album charts. It was still 1966.

That same year, Berry signed a group called Gladys Knight and the Pips. Gladys, the lead vocalist, was a Southern gospel singer whose voice had the shine of a copper penny glinting under the sun. Her brother Merald "Bubba" Knight and their cousins Edward Patten and William Guest were the Pips, who sang backup.

Like the Temptations, Gladys and her family got off to a slow start at Motown until Norman stepped up and wrote a hit song titled "I Heard It Through the Grapevine."

The song was called "Grapevine" within the Motown offices. Norman had produced the song with Marvin Gaye as its singer. He presented the song at one of Hitsville's Friday morning meetings.

At the same meeting, H-D-H presented a song also sung by Marvin, titled "Your Unchanging Love." The two songs were put to a vote. The group was asked to choose which one of the songs they felt would be a hit. The majority voted for "Grapevine." Usually, at the Friday meetings, the majority vote won.

But this time Berry overrode the vote. He chose "Your Unchanging Love" as the next Motown song to be recorded with big-hit potential, because he believed it was a better choice for Marvin's mastery of romantic songs.

Norman made a strong appeal at the meeting. He told the group that "Grapevine" gave him chills whenever he heard it, and that chills meant he could *feel* a hit song. Norman's chills didn't change Berry's mind. He stood firm. "Your Unchanging Love" was the winner. The song did well, but by Motown's mega-success standards, it was a moderate hit that peaked at number thirty-three on the *Billboard* Hot 100 list.

Meanwhile, Norman's persistence went into overdrive. For months, he kept bugging Berry about "Grapevine," urging him to reconsider the song. Berry kept saying no. Norman would not give up. One day, he even followed Berry to Detroit's 20 Grand nightclub, where Berry had gone to unwind. He begged Berry to allow him to present "Grapevine" again, but with a different recording artist singing the vocals. Berry was so sick and tired of Norman asking about "Grapevine" that he agreed.

Norman recorded the song with Gladys Knight and the Pips. He rearranged "Grapevine" so that it had a more up-tempo beat and also in a way that featured Gladys's bold gospel vocal style.

He presented the song at Hitsville's Friday morning meeting again. This time, Berry couldn't deny "Grapevine." Everyone at the meeting was impressed with the song and how Norman had given it a whole new tonal hue.

"I Heard It Through the Grapevine" initially sold 2.5 million copies and has since sold millions more. When it was released in 1967, it was Motown's best-selling single of all time. That grapevine grew like a healthy plant, winding its way to the top of the music charts. It became a number two pop hit on the *Billboard* Hot 100 chart, and a *Billboard* number one R&B hit for six weeks.

The song was the breakthrough blockbuster Gladys and her family members needed. It established them as another of Motown's leading acts. And the song itself was so popular that a year later Motown released a version of "I Heard It Through the Grapevine" sung by Marvin Gaye, which became a number one pop hit for seven weeks.

By this time, Berry Gordy had, without a doubt, found the secret that gave Motown songs crossover appeal. It was music that struck an emotional chord. Motown songs were now fully embraced by all kinds of listeners.

Race music had become a thing of the past. The Motown sound was no longer defined by race. As Berry cited in the liner notes of *Greatest Hits (the Temptations Album)*, the Motown sound was now considered "The Sound of Young America."

Gladys Knight and the Pips were a family act from Atlanta, Georgia, that stepped into Motown's lineup of groups with smooth dance routines. Their footwork showed off choreography by Hitsville dance instructor Cholly Atkins. They had a large following for their live performances, but had to work hard to score a hit record.

We've been driving a while, child. By most counts, we should be weary. But I can see by your wide-open eyes and that smile that you are far from sleepy.

So look out the window and check out the stars. They're bright enough to light our way. If you look real good, you can make out the names of the singers and hits that are still big at this point in our trip:

Marvin Gaye's star is high with "How Sweet It Is (To Be Loved by You)" and "Ain't That Peculiar."

There's Martha and the Vandellas topping the charts with "Nowhere to Run."

You see the star that's pulsating? The one that's got its own special glow? That's Stevie Wonder, who's dropped "Little" from his name and is lighting up the night (and the airwaves) with a song called "Uptight (Everything's Alright)."

The Four Tops are shining bright with "Standing in the Shadows of Love."

And look—over there. It's as pretty as the Big Dipper. It's the Marvelettes singing "Don't Mess with Bill," another sparkling hit.

Baby, with all that twinkling and Motown glow above our heads, you might think things can't get any brighter on this Hitsville rhythm trip. Believe it or not, there's more star shine up ahead.

SINGING SUPREME

WOULD YOU LOOK AT THAT, CHILD?

I knew we'd come up on one sooner or later.

A STOP sign.

You can always spot a STOP sign from way down the road.

Maybe it's the bright red color that stands out from the rest.

Maybe it's that undeniable octagon shape.

Maybe it's those bold letters that can't be missed.

Whatever it is, we know a STOP sign when we see one.

And we stop.

And we take a good look.

And we respect the STOP.

This is what Berry Gordy did whenever he came upon someone whose uniqueness inspired him.

The Primettes were four girls with big pearls and even bigger dreams. Left to right, Betty McGlown, Diane Ross, Mary Wilson, and Florence Ballard. After they'd won fifteen dollars in prize money at a local talent contest, they were eager for a record deal. When the friends first auditioned for Berry Gordy, he told them they were too inexperienced to be recording artists.

He stopped.

And looked.

And considered where to go from there.

When a group of high school girls had first shown up at Hitsville in 1960 hoping to be discovered, one of them made Berry stop.

And look.

And consider.

It was her singular beauty that caught his attention.

She and her friends had formed a singing group called the Primettes. There were four of them—Florence "Flo" Ballard, Betty McGlown, Mary Wilson, and the gawkiest one of them all, a tenth grader named Diane Ross.

Diane and her classmates spent all of their after-school time at Hitsville, volunteering for any job that needed to be done. If somebody was looking for backup singers, the Primettes stepped forward. If the Funk Brothers wanted to add hand claps as musical accompaniment, the girls did their best R&B clapping in the hopes that they'd be invited into the recording studio to sing.

Day after day, they begged Berry to give them their big break or to at least let them audition for Motown.

Day after day, Berry told them to come back after they'd finished school.

Day after day, they showed up at Motown at three thirty in the afternoon, telling Berry they'd finished school—for *that day*.

Diane was the most persistent of the group. She was scrawny and awkward, but in Berry's eyes, she was the most beautiful. He didn't tell Diane at the time, but he also believed she had the potential to become one of the biggest stars in Motown's history, and in the world.

He agreed to sign the Primettes to a Motown recording contract. But there were conditions. First, they had to change their name to the Supremes. Soon after the group got its new name, Barbara Martin left to have a baby, so the newly formed quartet was down to three singers.

Even with their new name, Berry could see that the teenagers still needed intense priming. Flo, Mary, and Diane were far from supreme. These girls had grown up in the housing projects of Detroit. They were rough around the edges. The word *finesse* wasn't in their vocabulary. The Supremes needed an *extreme* makeover. They showed promise, but they weren't ready for prime time. As part of their agreement with Motown, the Supremes were required to take rigorous classes with Maxine Powell, not just twice a week like the other Motown acts, but daily. It was Maxine's job to turn these rough-cut teens into treasures by giving them her lessons in etiquette, posture, and grooming.

They also had to agree to work with the H-D-H songwriting team, who would develop material particularly suited to the silky singing style of this trio.

With Maxine's polishing and the songwriting skills of H-D-H, the Supremes began to live up to their name. Soon, they *were* supreme. Their song "Where Did Our Love Go" went to the Top 40 in just a few weeks.

Once Holland-Dozier-Holland started writing songs for the Supremes, the H-D-H in their names could have stood for "Hits-Do-Hit." After the success of "Where Did Our Love Go," their hits *did* hit—again and again and again.

Between 1964 and 1965, they wrote and produced four consecutive number one songs for the Supremes: "Baby Love," "Come See About Me," "Back in My Arms Again," and a song that was as singular and as special as a bright octagon on the horizon.

When the Supremes performed their hit "Stop! In the Name of Love," they showed audiences how to bring the song alive with Cholly Atkins's storytelling choreography, which was always a showstopper.

"Stop! In the Name of Love!" showcased the Supremes' style and grace.

And it made America stop and fall in love with the Supremes.

One of the best parts about stopping in the name of love was the choreography the Supremes brought to the song.

They didn't just *sing* "Stop!"—they showed it.

Honey child, now it's your turn to enjoy every stop of your own *stop*!

Put your hand up like you're halting traffic. Really flick your wrist, kid. Because stopping in the name of love needs to be strong.

Now, as the song says, "before you break my heart," cross both arms over your heart.

Keep them there.

Give yourself a little hug.

Sway.

Look up to the sky, sideways, like you're thinking it over.

Yeah, that's it, child. You're stopping. You're a star.

Every time I hear "Stop! In the Name of Love," I do what Berry Gordy did when he met Diane Ross and her friends.

I stop, child. Yes, *I* stop.

And I consider what I've come to know about Motown's premier female trio:

If chocolate pudding could sing, it would sound like the Supremes.

If you asked a jeweler to come up with a name for his new line of diamonds, he would call it "the Supremes."

If velvet and chiffon got together and had a baby-love, they could name it "Supremes."

That's how smooth and beautiful they were, sweetie.

That's how much they shimmered.

Whenever the Supremes performed, it was a Motown dream coming true in sequined Technicolor.

H-D-H rode their mega-hit-making wave, and created seven more Supremes Top 10s over the next six years. Five of these became number one songs on various *Billboard* charts.

If the Supremes' songs were a counting lesson, they'd be a study in the number one.

#1—"You Can't Hurry Love"
#1—"You Keep Me Hangin' On"
#1—"Love Is Here and Now You're Gone"
#1—"The Happening"
#1—"I Hear a Symphony"

With this kind of hits-do-hit success, Berry was eager to gain even greater recognition for the Supremes. Though they had gained tremendous mainstream appeal, he envisioned more widespread crossover attention for the group.

To achieve this, Berry believed Diane should be singled out. He insisted she change her name to *Diana*, which sounded more glamorous. He then began to mold Diana Ross into the ultimate star.

Berry had huge aspirations for Diana. He wanted to turn her into a pop-music diva.

While the girls continued to work on their stage presence in Maxine's classes at Hitsville, Diana was also sent to the John Robert Powers School for Social Grace, a finishing school in downtown Detroit, where she was one of the only black students.

John was charged with refining everything about Diana's offstage persona—her posture, gestures, speaking voice, smile—so that she appealed to white people as well as African Americans, and could continue Motown's crossover success.

FAMILY DRAMA

ALL RIGHT, HERE'S WHERE THE ROAD SWERVES.

Soon Berry was receiving calls and telegrams from Europe, requesting the Supremes. By the late 1960s, the Supremes had become as popular as the British singing sensation the Beatles. When Dusty Springfield, a British pop star, hosted a 1965 television special from London called *The Sound of Motown*, Berry, the Supremes, the Temptations, the Four Tops, Martha and the Vandellas, and the Miracles took their popularity to international heights.

I wish you could have seen it, kid. It was a beautiful sight. Watching those Motown performers gracing the land of fish and chips and potted ham filled me with pride.

Between you and me, my royal groove sources tell me that even the folks at Buckingham Palace crowded around the TV to watch *The Sound of Motown*.

The Motown singers also embarked on their first transatlantic tour, an

When Motown's singers went on an international tour, Paris eagerly welcomed the Supremes. Smiling in front of the Eiffel Tower was a dream come true for these beauties who'd grown up on the concrete sidewalks and city streets of Detroit. Though the Motown performers traveled as a group, Diana Ross got the most attention.

international traveling rendition of the Motortown Revue, now called the Motown Revue. They traveled through Great Britain, Germany, Holland, and France.

Everywhere the revue went, the Supremes garnered the most attention. All the Motown acts were well received, but the European press had a special fondness for Diana, who had gone from a Detroit duckling to an international black swan adored by everyone. Diana had tremendous drive to succeed and was eager to be famous.

Along with the international media's fascination with Diana, they were captivated by Berry Gordy, too. He could do no wrong, it seemed. People started calling him "the magic man" and "the star maker."

Well, when the magic man and his stars returned to Detroit, the Motown family fairy tale started to turn ugly. It's true, child, that in every family, people disagree. And, if I'm being completely honest, families do more than that—families fight. Let's just admit it. Let's say it how it really is. There are days when you want to throw down your brother or sister or cousin, or your best friend that you've known since nursery school, because they do something that makes you mad. Or because they get something you want or feel you deserve. Or because, plain and simple, they bug you.

This started to happen within the Motown family, mostly because Berry was lavishing all his attention on Diana and focusing less on the career needs and development of the other Motown family members.

Hitsville U.S.A. was beginning to lose its close-knit family feeling. People were angry. They were stressed out from so much traveling. Petty jealousies arose.

Martha Reeves was sick of walking through the halls of Hitsville hearing *Diana, Diana, Diana.* The Vandellas started to suffer a bad case of Supreme envy, especially as their Motown recording sessions decreased. Martha started to become depressed. She and the Vandellas left Motown.

The Temptations also plunged into problems. David Ruffin, the pretty boy with the cute eyeglasses, ignored Berry's Motown family rule about not drinking and using drugs. David suffered from drug and alcohol abuse that some say was sparked by the demands of fame and his own ego. As the lead singer, he wanted the group to change its name to "David Ruffin and the Temptations." He started to show up late, or not at all, to rehearsals and performances. The other Temptations kicked him out of the group and replaced him with Dennis Edwards from the Contours.

Even the Supremes began to unravel. Flo and Mary had also had enough of Diana, and Berry's devotion to her. Flo also broke the no-drinking Motown family rule. She started drinking heavily and was replaced by Diana's friend Cindy Birdsong.

In spring 1967, Berry decided that the group would be called "Diana Ross and the Supremes," and that Diana would be the headline singer.

The mounting tensions at Motown had pushed Marvin Gaye to a snapping point, too. He and Berry started to disagree and argue about things like how songs should be produced and what was best for Marvin's career. Marvin called Berry names behind his back. "Magic man" wasn't one of them.

Further weakening Motown's family unity, Berry moved his office out of the bungalow on West Grand Boulevard to a ten-story high-rise building in downtown Detroit.

In his new office, Berry tried to rise above the dissension in his company, but he couldn't fully escape the unrest that was happening in the streets below and in neighborhoods throughout America.

This was a heavy time, honey. Real heavy.

WHAT'S GOING ON

NOW, SWEETHEART, WE ARE CONTINUING INTO THE DARKNESS.

Please tighten your seat belt. Please keep a grip on your determination to stay with this journey.

Nobody wants to turn onto this road, but, like that ugly patch we passed where Emmett Till's body lay, and where those four little angels rest, this is necessary to our ride.

If you want to cover your eyes, then okay. But you must at least listen. You need to hear what's going on.

Because Motown was there through all of it.

To lift us up.

To keep us going.

To unite us, child.

Facing page: During the Detroit riots of 1967, the city burned with a fury so powerful, it was considered one of the most violent outbursts to ever happen in America.

To get us to the other side of sorrow.

As we go, I need you to know this isn't a short patch of sad. This part of the road stretches *on*. It'll be rough from 1967 to 1975.

All right, this is where our high beams can help. It's darker than dark on this road, and there are no stars out tonight.

Hold on. Here we go.

In the summer of 1967, the racial tension in the Motor City was as thick as the humidity. During the day, the oppressive heat choked the sunshine. At night, the stars drowned in the dark of this time period.

Do you smell something? I sure do. When there's trouble on the way, it has a foul odor.

This all started in the early morning hours of Sunday, July 23, 1967, when the Detroit police, who were mostly white, raided an African American nightclub on the city's west side.

Kid, *raid* is one of those tricky words that means different things to different people. In this instance, the police busted into the nightclub unannounced. Some say that the raid was racially motivated and that the white police were looking to rile the black citizens enough to start a fight that would give the cops a reason to arrest black people.

The men and women inside the club were celebrating the return of two young men who had just come home after serving in the Vietnam War, a war that was being fought between North Vietnam and the government of South Vietnam. In an attempt to keep communism from spilling over from North Vietnam to South Vietnam, the United States got involved in the war by sending American troops to fight. To this day, folks wonder why the United States stuck its nose into that conflict. It was complicated, child. Hard to understand. And real bad.

At the time the police raid happened, the war was at its height. Kids were in combat. They were far away from home. They were being forced to fight.

Many young people who had been drafted into military service said goodbye to their families and never returned home.

When the police showed up at the nightclub in Detroit, a race riot broke out. It was a fight between black citizens and white citizens.

Oh, child. Oh, oh, child. This wasn't just any riot. It was a massacre, beginning on that summer Sunday.

The disturbance started to build.

People hurled bottles and rocks.

Looting and fires ran through the streets.

Smoke filled Detroit's skyline.

Bullets were flung every which way.

Thieves and snipers ran wild.

Warnings of the riot's intensity spread quickly throughout Detroit.

Several Motown singers were performing at Detroit's Fox Theatre in the late afternoon of the same Sunday when the riot began.

Martha Reeves was onstage singing a song called "Jimmy Mack." Before Martha could get to the second refrain—"when are you comin' back?"—someone whispered that she needed to stop singing immediately and told her to instruct the audience to leave quietly because of trouble in the streets.

At the Fox Theatre in Detroit, Martha Reeves sang "Jimmy Mack," a song about a young recruit returning from war. At the same time, the streets outside erupted with looting, gunfire, and violence.

When people remember that time, many look back at how the Detroit race riot started. It began with innocent citizens rejoicing in the return of soldiers from war. I can't help but think about how Martha Reeves was performing a song asking her boyfriend, Jimmy, "When are you comin' back?"

Martha's plea was a prayer that your guy would come home soon from an overseas battlefield.

The Detroit riot lasted five days. It was one of the bloodiest, deadliest uprisings in America's history.

The worst part was the death toll. The killing of so many innocent people who died in the squalor, in the crossfire, child. Many lost their lives, most of them black citizens. The youngest to die was a four-year-old girl named Tanya Blanding.

Whew, this is hard going, I know. I'll pull over for a moment so we can catch our breath. You okay? No? Me neither. Whenever I pass this way, my stomach hurts. And something tugs at my throat. And I feel heavy. It's a shame, these horrible times.

I'm sorry to be the one to have to tell you this, but there's more loss up ahead. But we're together, and we're safe. And, thankfully, Motown is here to help us make sense of it all.

Let's keep going. This part will be over soon.

The Detroit riot was just one of many outbursts happening in towns and neighborhoods across America. People were angry about so much racial and social injustice. They lashed out by protesting, fighting, screaming to be heard.

Teenagers were especially conscious of racial inequality, as it affected their friendships and the way they dealt with their parents, who sometimes didn't agree with their views on the race situation in America.

Kids saw that one of the easiest ways to strike back against the adults they considered to be "the establishment" was to embrace fashions that aggravated their parents, teachers, preachers, and anybody else who was older than twenty-five.

For teens, the shorter the skirts, the better. The wider the flare on a pair of bell-bottom pants, the more the establishment shook their heads in disapproval.

This was how kids expressed their discontent with the violence and upheaval that was happening in the world around them.

Remember all those smooth, conked hairdos from earlier on our trip? Well, fried-and-dyed hair was being replaced by Afros as big as a sunrise. Kinky 'dos for boys and girls were now in style. For African Americans, wearing their hair natural rather than straightening it was a way to express their cultural identity. The Temptations were one of the first Motown groups to show their racial pride by growing their 'fros.

A raging heat of anger swelled in the United States. On April 4, 1968, Martin Luther King, Jr., was assassinated in Memphis, Tennessee. This ignited more riots in every major American city.

Oh, child. That was one of the most depressing days ever. A soul-sorry shame. Sadder than sad.

Things got worse, too. On June 6, 1968, Senator Robert F. Kennedy, a friend and supporter of Martin Luther King, Jr., and a firm believer in racial harmony, was also assassinated. Five years before that, Robert's brother, President John F. Kennedy, had been killed by an assassin on November 22, 1963.

With the world's peace leaders gone, people felt lost, disillusioned, afraid, irate.

Neighbors and friends asked one another how peace would ever stand a chance. Children buried their faces in their mama's and daddy's laps, crying about so much violence.

Rhythm riders always cry when we get to this part of the trip. But through Motown's powerful reach, the Sound of Young America was there to help. Motown released an album called *Free at Last*, a collection of speeches by Martin Luther King, Jr., which served as a loving tribute. With this album, along with Motown's previous release of *The Great March to Freedom*, Motown documented important moments in civil rights history.

Smokey Robinson and the Miracles let us all know we were not alone in our grief following the assassinations of America's most beloved leaders. Smokey and the Miracles recorded a song called "Abraham, Martin and John," a sorrowful folk ballad that honored the slain leaders—Abraham Lincoln, who, as America's sixteenth president, had ended slavery, Martin Luther King, Jr., and President John F. Kennedy.

The song expressed what so many of us couldn't say because we were too busy choking back our tears. The lyrics, written by Dick Holler, reminded us of a sad truth: "it seems the good die young." The Miracles' recording became a Top 40 hit single in 1969.

Motown was there to shine its light in the darkest times. There to ease the way. We needed this comfort, child. We needed something to help us understand what made no sense.

When I look back at those days, it makes me proud to be the Groove. 'Cause you see, the Groove is most alive when souls ache. I was there when mothers cried at the loss of their sons. Through my rhythm, I kept their broken hearts beating. I kept faith's flame on the front burner when despair tried to take over.

Remember Norman Whitfield, that pesky kid who hung around Motown waiting for the chance to write a song? Well, by this time, Norman was a grown man with some big ideas. He paired his talent with singer-songwriter Barrett Strong, who had been the vocalist on Motown's "Money" single, and Edwin Starr, a Motown singer who hadn't yet established himself as a well-known talent.

These guys called on the Groove to bring a pounding tempo to their song titled "War," a hard-hitting protest of the conflict in Vietnam.

You gotta hear this song, kid. It slams at you. It makes you think. It helps you shout back at so much senselessness. You can't just sing along with "War," you have to proclaim its lyrics. You have to pump a fist, high and hard at the song's refrain.

There's no glory in war that I can see, but something beautiful happened after "War" was recorded and released. It didn't prevent the war from continuing, but the song struck a chord with so many listeners that I like to believe "War" helped angry people put their rage in a good place. By voicing the song's protest, they could tuck their fury into rhythm's pocket. "War" helped us step back from inflicting our pain onto others, as all of us prayed for the trouble in Vietnam to end. In 1970, "War" became a number one hit on the *Billboard* Hot 100 chart.

As more soldiers lost their lives, it was a busy season for undertakers and headstone carvers. We wanted to put the hearse in reverse but couldn't stop the dying. "War" expressed it so well.

Marvin Gaye was deeply troubled by the race riots, assassinations, and so much other violence that troubled America.

When Marvin's brother, Frankie, returned from the war, Marvin went to visit him at their parents' home in Washington, D.C. Right away, Marvin could see that Frankie was different. The war had changed him. Frankie told Marvin about the violence he'd seen, about the fears and nightmares the war had plagued him with. Marvin and Frankie stayed up most of the night talking, crying, hugging, and wiping their tears. Marvin made a promise to his brother. He would use his music to express the despair they felt and to offer some kind of solace to others who were also feeling hopeless and overwhelmed.

Marvin called Berry in the Bahamas, where Berry was on vacation, and told him that he wanted to produce a protest record. Berry thought this was a terrible idea. He scolded Marvin and hung up the phone. But Marvin was determined.

He wrote a soulful, passionate song called "What's Going On" that spoke to the strife of the times.

Kid, the early 1970s in America were filled with so much conflict. It was like a blinding curtain that refused to lift.

"What's Going On" gently pulled back that curtain to let us view it all. It

Marvin Gaye wrote and sang songs that reflected the pain of war, police brutality, and other troubles of the early 1970s. His song "What's Going On" used chords found in jazz, gospel, and classical music. It remains one of Motown's most popular songs, and still has relevance today.

showed us mothers and fathers crying. Sons and brothers dying. So much cruelty and pain.

The song stares us straight in the eye and urges us to look for ways to move past hostility.

Marvin presented the song to Berry, who hated it. So did the Motown team at the Friday morning quality-control meeting. Everyone worried the song was too hard-hitting, too political. They were convinced nobody would buy the record. Even though Motown had released recordings of the speeches of Martin Luther King, Jr., and the song "War," they believed people now wanted more of Motown's light, happy dance songs to offset times filled with so much dissension.

Harry Balk and Barney Ales, executives at Motown, disagreed. They helped Marvin get the song released without telling Berry. In January 1971, 100,000 copies of the record sold immediately. Harry and Barney manufactured 100,000 more records, which also sold right away.

"What's Going On" quickly became Motown's fastest-selling single at that time. It peaked at number one on the Hot Soul Singles chart, and at number two on the *Billboard* Hot 100 chart.

Berry Gordy was surprised when he learned of the song's success. But he couldn't turn his back on what was going on around him. People wanted this song. They *needed* it.

The impact of the "What's Going On" single inspired Marvin to create an entire album titled *What's Going On*.

He envisioned what he called a "concept album," which would include songs told from a Vietnam War veteran's point of view after he'd come home to America, where he saw that serving his country hadn't helped improve injustice, poverty, suffering, or crime.

Although the "What's Going On" single had received such a positive reception, Berry thought the concept album was a big mistake. He refused to let Marvin release it.

Marvin put it to Berry straight. If Berry didn't allow him to release the album, Marvin would never record another Motown song again. Barry relented. As soon as the *What's Going On* album hit stores in May 1971, people lined up to purchase it.

I guess this proved that even though Berry had great instincts for the kinds of records that would appeal to people, he wasn't right about everything. "What's Going On" taught him a valuable lesson in humility, and that it was a good idea to remain teachable.

Child, do you see the light coming up ahead on the road?

111

Do you see the sun starting to rise? It's a beautiful sight, child. That bleak mist curtain is giving way to a new day. It's rolling back, kid, disappearing so that you and the Groove can drive clear on through.

We can thank Marvin Gaye's determination and virtuosity for that. The nine songs on his album spoke to our humanity, our chance for a bright future. *What's Going On* celebrated the goodness and charity of the human soul. It would become Motown's bestselling album of all time, is considered by historians to be one of the greatest albums ever made, and is the first Motown album to credit the Funk Brothers for their jazz-gospel-classical orchestration.

Hey, check out that sign, child.

It's pointing us to hope's highway.

Prepare to Exit

Vietnam War will end—April 1975

Merge to Next Ramp—J-5

TCB, ABC, 1-2-3-4-5

THIS, KID, IS WHERE THE ROAD SPLITS.

One side is lined with palm trees and movie stars. The other is filled with homegrown talent and family ties.

Both roads are worth taking. And so, you and I are going to travel down each of them. I'm glad our gas tank still has plenty of fuel, 'cause in this part of our journey, Motown covers a lot of ground.

Look to the left, child. There's Detroit after all that rioting. When all those brothers and sons have come home from Vietnam, battle-weary. After so much discord in Hitsville's harmony.

In Berry's eyes, his hometown had become a broken place. The sheen from its past was starting to turn ashy.

Now look to your right. We'll head down *that* road, toward the hot, blue sky. To sidewalks paved in granite. To glamour everywhere you glance.

This is Hollywood, honey. It's not just the palm trees and star-studded sidewalks that let you know we're not in Detroit anymore. You can tell by the cars. Everybody's driving convertibles with their tops down. They say it never rains in this place.

Here, on Hollywood Boulevard, cars are sleek bucket-seaters that come in colors named after tropical fruits: mango Mustang, pineapple Porsche, lemon Lamborghini. They say everyone on this boulevard is famous or on the way to becoming a household name.

Hollywood was very attractive to Berry. At the very end of the 1960s, he had started making plans to move Motown to Los Angeles. He wanted to take his company to sunnier heights by expanding Motown into a full-scale entertainment venture that included television specials and motion pictures. Berry also wanted to bring new talent and fresh ideas to build on his existing lineup of talent.

Though Berry retained property in Detroit and kept some of his staff in the Motor City, his sights were now set on making it big in the land of swimming pools and movie stars.

In California, Berry established a division called Motown Productions, which created television specials featuring Motown artists. He paired two of Motown's hottest groups, Diana Ross and the Supremes and the Temptations, and produced a nationally televised special called *TCB—Taking Care of Business: Diana Ross and the Supremes with the Temptations*.

When Diana and her ladies came onto the screen in swirled, sequined gowns, they were *refined*, child, sophisticated. Then, here came the Temptations, so suave, and dressed in satin suits as glistening green as lime Jell-O.

The eight singers filled the hour with musical classics and romantic ballads, including their joint hit, "I'm Gonna Make You Love Me," a song they recorded in 1968 together that instantly became a Top 10 hit.

A full orchestra backed them up, adding to the class act. Before the opening credits for the *TCB* show, a voice-over announcer for the NBC network told viewers, "The following program is brought to you in living color."

Yes, that's right. Color was alive and well and living large that evening. *TCB* was watched by millions of viewers of all races. It was billed as the first major black television special in history, and it was another example of Motown's crossover appeal. This was a proud step for Berry and for Motown.

Speaking of pride-stepping, do you know how to *bo-dip*?

Yeah, that's right, bo-dip. It's when your Afro pick is sitting proud in your

Diana Ross and the Supremes and the Temptations took care of business as they dazzled viewers on *TCB*, a television musical review that featured show tunes, Motown hits, and ballads. It exceeded network expectations and became America's top-rated variety show of 1968.

back pocket, and you look so sly that you can't help but bo-dip while walking down the street. When you bo-dip, make sure to really bend your knees when you walk, and let one hand trail behind you like you've got a puppy on a leash.

You're gonna need to bo-dip for the next part of this trip. Up ahead, we're about to enter into the 1970s, where the Groove was everywhere, and when it was all about being *groovy*.

While Berry worked in Hollywood, Motown still had its roots back in Detroit. A new Motown employee was holding it down at Hitsville U.S.A. Suzanne de Passe was a college-age kid from Harlem whom Berry had hired to be his executive assistant.

Suzanne was whip smart, quick-witted, hardworking, and intuitive. She arranged for five brothers from Gary, Indiana, to have an audition at Motown.

The Jackson brothers had started their careers by performing in small-town talent contests and nightspots. These boys had star quality so bright you needed sunglasses to watch them. They were so hip that only a bo-dip with platform shoes would do whenever you listened to their music. Gladys Knight had already told Berry about the brothers and had suggested he sign them up.

Jackie, Tito, Jermaine, and Marlon Jackson were teenagers whose charisma was a magnet for pulling in fans. But it was their younger brother and lead singer, Michael, whose allure was electric. Michael Jackson was a ten-year-old exploding with talent.

Suzanne called Berry in Hollywood, urging him to come see the Jacksons perform. As soon as Suzanne told Berry the brothers ranged in age from ten to seventeen, Berry was quick to say no thanks. After navigating the child-labor-law restrictions for Little Stevie Wonder, and the list of requirements issued by Stevie's mother, Berry was not eager to deal with five more kids.

Berry stayed in Hollywood while Suzanne auditioned the Jacksons at Hitsville. She filmed them performing "I Got the Feelin'," a song made famous by

R&B singer James Brown. On the tape, Michael was out front singing, working dance moves so slick they put a gleam on Motown's studio floor.

The segment Suzanne filmed was black and white, choppy, and out of focus. But, honey, that didn't matter. Michael Jackson *got the feelin'* every time he belted James Brown's refrain—"baby, baby, baby, c'mon!"

And, baby, you couldn't help but *c'mon* when you watched the Jackson brothers bring their twinkle to the camera. When Berry viewed the video from his Hollywood office, *he* came *on* with a recording contract for the Jacksons. He also named them The Jackson 5. It was 1968.

The brothers moved to Los Angeles. They stayed with Berry until their parents, Joseph and Katherine, could join them and find a house where the Jackson family could all live.

The Jackson 5 didn't just sing. They lit up the stage with hipper-than-hip costumes and choreography. And, oh, those 'fros! Here, they bring their J-5 shine. Left to right, Tito, Marlon, Michael, Jackie, and Jermaine.

Berry and Suzanne put Motown's marketing muscle behind these kids. They came up with the idea to have Diana Ross introduce The Jackson 5 to the world, which she did on August 11, 1969, at a Beverly Hills club called the Daisy. A few weeks later, the Jacksons appeared on television, where they sang at the Black Miss America pageant in New York City's Madison Square Garden.

Once America was introduced to the Jackson kids, the group became unstoppable. Their first hit was a song called "I Want You Back," released at the end of 1969.

Michael and his brothers sure knew how to sell that song. Whenever they performed "I Want You Back," they went onto the stage with sunrise Afros, fringe dripping from bell-bottoms, and chunk-heeled bo-dips that were so groovy.

Michael's songbird solo let everybody know all he wanted—all he *needed*—was one more chance to show his darlin' that he'd been blind to let her fly out of his arms.

And, honey, when ten-year-old Michael winked right into the TV camera that had zoomed in for his close-up, every girl in the world *was* his darlin'.

"I Want You Back" became a number one hit in January 1970. The song set a record. Michael Jackson became the first person born after *Billboard* magazine had established the Hot 100 list to reach the number one spot on the *Billboard* Hot 100 Pop Singles chart.

Fans started calling the Jackson brothers "J-5," and they chanted Michael's nickname—"MJ! MJ! MJ!"

The Jackson 5 were like points of light on a very bright star. The brothers each had their own special sparkle. Together, as a group, they created a hit-making sensation that ignited a galaxy of musical styles—R&B, soul, funk, pop, rock, and love songs—and also lit up television and live stage performances. These boys had everything Motown needed to build the company's Hollywood

Motown and the Jacksons were a golden combination. Motown made the most of the group's phenomenal success. The company put big marketing dollars behind the brothers, whose faces appeared on the covers of teen magazines and coloring books and on lunch boxes and board games.

presence. They were cute, wholesome, smoother than peanut butter. Their up-beat style shook off the low-down feelings that had festered as a result of the Vietnam War and America's social unrest.

In 1970, the brothers introduced a song on *American Bandstand*, a television show for teenagers that featured bands playing and teenagers dancing to popular music. The Jacksons' song was called "ABC." That song sent TV to grade school, sat at the teacher's desk, and taught America to read.

As soon as "ABC" was released, kids everywhere couldn't wait to learn their letters, the J-5 way.

"ABC" was an R&B alphabet party. Its lyrics sang the praises of reading, writing, and arithmetic, and it let us all know that the branches of the learning tree are worth reaching for.

But, as the Jacksons reminded us, if you can't spell *me* and *you*, and if you can't add us together like one plus one equals two, then your education is missing something everybody needs to learn—love.

It's that simple, child. All you gotta do is open a book, recite the alphabet's first three letters, and shake it, shake it, baby!

"ABC" became an instant hit that rocketed the Jacksons to more record-breaking fame. They became one of the few groups in the history of recorded music to have their first four major label singles—"I Want You Back," "ABC," "The Love You Save," and "I'll Be There"—reach the top of the *Billboard* Hot 100.

The Jackson brothers put a high five on their hit wave by becoming the characters on a Saturday morning cartoon series called *The Jackson 5ive*, which first aired in September 1971. The television show featured the brothers as animated youngsters who got themselves into funny scrapes but who always came out on top singing. A cartoon version of Berry Gordy was the adult on the show, which also featured animated animal characters based on Michael's real-life pets.

Berry didn't realize it then, but his bestseller assembly line was slowing its roll. Between you and me, kid, even though Berry didn't know it, the Jackson 5 would be among the last megastars to come out of his hit-making factory machine.

NEW DIRECTIONS

I'VE TAKEN PASSENGERS LIKE YOU ON THIS RIDE AT LEAST A HUNDRED TIMES.

With each and every trip, I'm reminded that Hollywood was a long way from Hitsville U.S.A. Whenever I pull onto the LA freeway, I can't help but wonder how Berry had planned to keep his Detroit Motown roots firmly planted while, at the same time, spreading his wings over the Hollywood Hills.

As it turns out, with a company split between two places, the Motown family tree started to lose its leaves. Berry had purchased a mansion and now spent most of his time in California focusing his attention on ventures such as filmmaking and television.

He and Diana Ross fell in love and had a daughter together. Berry still had big career dreams for Diana and was putting his heart and soul into making her an even bigger superstar. As a result, the Supremes broke up, and Diana pursued a solo career. With Diana's future in mind, Berry formed Motown

Berry Gordy and Diana Ross became romantically involved. He focused his attention on making Diana into a worldwide sensation. She became his protégé, following every step of his career advice.

Productions, a film division of his company. He financed Motown's first major motion picture, *Lady Sings the Blues*, a movie about the life and times of jazz singer Billie Holiday. Diana starred in the film, playing the role of Lady Day.

The movie's screenplay was written by Suzanne de Passe and Chris Clark, another Motown employee. Suzanne and Chris received an Academy Award nomination for best screenplay. Diana was nominated for an Academy Award for best actress. Berry had created a multimillion-dollar African American–owned media company, had turned Diana Ross into a worldwide star, and had reached the heights of crossover success in music, television, and movies.

Back in Detroit, Motown's recording artists began to feel slighted. One by one, the original hit makers started to leave the company to record on other labels that paid them more money than they were earning at Motown. These companies also promised to make their careers a priority, something several Motown performers felt was no longer happening at Motown.

As the 1970s progressed, Berry got goodbye calls and farewell letters from Martha Reeves and the Vandellas, the Four Tops, the Temptations, the H-D-H songwriting team, songwriter Norman Whitfield, and Gladys Knight and the Pips.

In 1976, the Jackson 5 left Motown and changed their name to "The Jacksons." Randy Jackson, their youngest brother, who was fourteen years old, replaced Jermaine Jackson, who stayed at Motown out of loyalty to Berry.

This was hard going for Berry. It was difficult for him to watch so many of the acts he'd built now recording for other companies. When Michael Jackson's solo album *Off the Wall* was released in 1979 by Epic Records, it sold 20 million copies worldwide. Three years later, Michael's *Thriller* album became one of the world's bestselling albums of all time. Michael had gone from being a cute kid who could rock a 'fro to a global sensation whose flutter-gut vocals and moonwalk dance-glide had rocketed him to a dimension higher than the moon itself.

Okay, kid, here's where we can put the pedal to the metal. This part of the road heads into the 1980s. After losing so many of its top performers, Motown quickly started to roll in a new direction.

Marvin Gaye and Diana Ross left the company in 1981 to embark on careers with record labels that paid each of them millions of dollars to sign on. Honey, this was one of the saddest Motown moments for Berry Gordy. He'd spent so much time and creativity building Diana and Marvin, and now they were leaving Motown. It was like Berry's closest kin were turning their backs on the family that had nurtured them, raised them up, and given them wings to fly. Now they were flying away.

The Motown performers were hurt, too. They appreciated all that Berry had done to launch their careers but now felt slighted by what he wouldn't provide—bigger salaries and greater exposure they felt they deserved.

123

Michael Jackson achieved global success as "The King of Pop" when his *Thriller* album won a Grammy Award for Album of the Year and became one of the bestselling records of all time.

Fortunately, several performers remained loyal to Motown. After the Miracles broke up in 1978, Smokey Robinson moved to Los Angeles to work with Berry, helping him build Motown in California.

Stevie Wonder stayed at Motown, too, where he continued to write, record, and produce hits that ranged from ballads to funk. Stevie developed as a music creator and social activist.

Stevie was one of the leaders in a campaign to make Martin Luther King, Jr.'s birthday a national holiday. In 1981, Stevie traveled to Washington, D.C., where, on January 15, he held the Rally for Peace press conference. Stevie made history when he spoke publicly on behalf of this cause. He wrote and recorded a Motown song called "Happy Birthday." The song pays homage to Martin Luther King, Jr. It tells listeners that a man who did so much good deserves a holiday named in his honor. And if you listen closely to Stevie's delivery of "Happy Birthday," you might hear him scolding lawmakers for not giving Martin Luther King, Jr., a fitting commemoration.

"Happy Birthday" became the theme song of Stevie's campaign. Soon, so many people were singing Stevie's rendition of "Happy Birthday" to Martin Luther King, Jr.'s, memory that politicians couldn't help but listen. On November 2, 1983, President Ronald Reagan signed a bill making Martin Luther King Day a federal holiday. The first official Martin Luther King Day was held on January 20, 1986.

One thing has always been true of Berry and Motown. They've kept my groove alive with the times. When disco music became popular, Motown developed beyond its R&B roots to meet disco lovers with music that made them want to dance. Berry led his company into the disco era by inviting new members to the Motown family throughout the 1980s. Groups such Lionel Richie and the Commodores and DeBarge, along with funk singers Rick James and Teena Marie, pumped Motown disco hits into dance clubs.

Back then, if you went to a disco spot singing the DeBarge hit "Rhythm of the Night," you could turn the party out by doing some of the most popular disco dance moves, such as the Giddy Down and the Bunny Slope.

If you called your lady a "Brick House"—also the name of the Commodores' hit song—you were giving her a compliment.

Or, if you followed Teena Marie's straightforward way of dealing with things, you'd be telling your guy you love him by talkin' "Square Biz."

It's good to have fun at a party, dancing under a disco ball. And it's a beautiful thing to express your affection for the one you love.

Stevie Wonder, who had grown up at Motown, stayed at the company when others were signing contracts with competing record labels. Stevie used his notoriety to galvanize people around political causes, such as the movement to make Martin Luther King, Jr.'s birthday a national commemoration. Later in his career, he was named a United Nations Messenger of Peace.

But, honey, do me a favor. If you really care about somebody, please don't sing Rick James's Top 40 hit "Super Freak" to her face, because your friend may not be too pleased when she hears Rick's refrain, which claims that "pretty kinky" is a good thing.

Don't get me wrong, I love Rick's hard-driving beat. But although he sings the praises of his woman as being special "from her head down to her toenails," some people may not appreciate Rick's "Super Freak" way of paying tribute.

Motown's disco performers recorded most of their songs in California. Berry still owned his offices on West Grand Boulevard in Detroit, but Hitsville U.S.A. had become a place of Motown's past.

THE GROOVE GOES ON

WHEN I WAS A NEW GROOVE, NOT MUCH OLDER THAN YOU ARE NOW, I WAS STILL FINDING MY BEAT.

But in time, I learned an important lesson. I figured out that it's a good idea to stop the music when you get tired. That's what happened to Berry Gordy. After so many performers left Motown, his company started to lose money. At the same time, Berry started to lose his passion for what was once a golden enterprise. The most exciting years of Hitsville U.S.A. were gone. Berry no longer enjoyed overseeing the business he'd started nearly thirty years before.

In 1988, Berry sold portions of Motown to MCA Records for $61 million. As part of the deal, MCA would own rights to the Motown name, the Motown record catalog, and whatever remained of Motown recording artists' contracts. Berry held on to Motown's film and television production company. He also kept the publishing rights to most of Motown's top-selling songs, which, in 1997, he sold to EMI Music Publishing for $132 million.

Berry's sale of Motown reminds me of another lesson I've learned along the way. When you let go of one beat, a new tempo often comes in and taps you on the shoulder.

In the years soon after Berry sold Motown, he and several Hitsville U.S.A. artists received the highest honors bestowed in the entertainment industry. Berry Gordy, the Supremes, the Temptations, Stevie Wonder, the Four Tops, H-D-H, and Gladys Knight and the Pips were inducted into the Rock and Roll Hall of Fame. (Smokey Robinson had been inducted in 1987.)

On October 24, 1996, Johnny Grant, the honorary mayor of Hollywood, presented Berry with a star on the Hollywood Walk of Fame.

Since then, Berry has been walking proud in the glory of Motown's legacy. The bungalow he purchased at 2648 West Grand Boulevard in Detroit is now a museum that keeps the Motown sound alive with displays of Hitsville U.S.A. memorabilia.

A Broadway show called *Motown: The Musical* brought "Dancing in the Street" and all kinds of sweet Motown memories to thousands of fans both old and new.

So much else has happened, too. So many events that point to Motown's impact on our world. Just as Motown was always there to inspire us, to lift us up, to help us march past struggle—to change us—those unforgettable songs are still lifting us to great heights.

On February 24, 2011, President Barack Obama celebrated the music of Motown at a special White House concert featuring Stevie Wonder and Smokey Robinson. President Obama called Motown's music "the sound track of the civil rights era."

That sound track is a beautiful halo of light spreading its radiance around the sun. Do you see it up there on the horizon? It's that orange-soda circle sinking low behind the trees.

Here comes dusk. Soon the stars will make their crisscross journeys in the sky. When you look at those stars now, you'll view them differently. You'll know those flickering lights are memories, child.

You see, even though our Rhythm Ride has come to an end, it's the memories, and the promise of tomorrow, that keep our journey going.

And, if I may say so myself, it's the Groove that continues to move this trip forward. Without me steering, there would *be* no beat. Without the Groove running deep, R&B, soul, funk, pop, and the blues would have no heat.

But praises be to Motown's dream. 'Cause it's the Sound of Young America pumping *its* beat. It's the unforgettable pulse keeping hope and joy alive. It's the music of Motown that never dies.

Smokey Robinson and Berry Gordy share a hug and lots of good memories. Their friendship, talent, determination, and hard work changed American music forever.

Author's Note

Through Motown, we are all members of the same family, drawn together by a common thread of melodies and lyrics that have moved us, made us smile, helped us fall in love, and given us the strength to walk through painful times.

In writing the Motown story, I was struck by Berry Gordy's ability to create a business that lets us share a collective experience.

My parents, Gwen and Phil Davis, circa mid-1960s at a Washington, D.C., nightclub. She's nineteen and he's twenty-two. He's about to ask her to marry him and will pop the question after singing his a cappella rendition of the Temptations' "My Girl." In preparation for this special evening, his sweetheart spent several hours styling her hair to look like one of the Supremes.

That was Berry's magic. Motown's music captivates listeners of all races and social classes. Its staying power has become an unparalleled legacy. Also, Motown is a distinguished African American family-owned enterprise that has opened doors to racial equality while delivering a product that never fails to make us happy.

Motown's musical roots reach back to the drums of Mother Africa, Negro spirituals, gospel, jazz, and the blues. It is part of a musical heritage that speaks to the progress of African American people.

Throughout Motown's history, there were several Motown record labels, often named after Berry Gordy's family members. Songs were recorded on these various labels, though they all came under the Motown umbrella. For the sake of simplicity, the recordings cited in this book are primarily referred to as Motown songs.

Rhythm Ride started as a simple informational book, then grew into a testimony to the heart and soul of black music. As I wrote, the book became a family tribute, a social history, and a praise party all rolled into one package. It also turned into a love song that expresses my admiration for an era of R&B, soul, funk, pop, and ballads that changed the face of music forever. And that's why, for me, the writing of this book is a celebration.

To contextualize the music, I found it important to include aspects of the social and political climate of the times, and how Motown responded to and influenced these.

I chose to render Motown's story as a road trip, told from the point of view of "the Groove," an elder entity whose voice is that of someone who's traveled the journey to Motown's development.

The voice of the Groove is modeled after that of James K. Snowden, Jr., my second cousin, who everybody in our family calls "Scoopy."

Scoopy started his career as a small-town teen deejay, then worked his way to becoming a radio professional in major markets such as Detroit, New York, New Orleans, and Houston. Scoopy was one of the notable African Americans working in the field of radio who served up music on platters so hot they could sizzle a steak.

As his career progressed, he became a sought-after voice-over actor and music industry executive. Scoopy's notoriety is legendary at Davis family reunions. Some families brag about the doctors, lawyers, teachers, or ministers in their family trees. For the Davises, Scoopy's accomplishments rank right up there with the most prestigious medical and law degrees, and with hard-earned PhDs in education and theology.

As a veteran of the record business, Scoopy possesses the same qualities required of a lawyer, doctor, teacher, or preacher. He's smart, thoughtful, and articulate.

My cousin can "talk music." He knows everything about the origins of black song and instrumentals. He can reel off information about the nuances of musical genres and black singer-songwriters. And the man can tell some stories. Good stories from his life as a kid deejay, dubbed "Dr. Soul" and "The Snowman" on New York's WBLS radio.

While there are many books and documentaries about the history of Motown, few speak directly to today's young readers whose parents and grandparents experienced Motown's music for the very first time and were kids themselves when Berry Gordy's hit-making machine was coming alive.

That's why the adaptation of Scoopy's vernacular is so important in telling the Motown story. My cousin has experienced key moments in the history of black entertainment that the rest of us can only dream of. He's got the inside track on the performers who started as teen wannabes from the neighborhood and became legends.

Scoopy's spent time hanging out with Smokey Robinson, the Jackson 5, Diana Ross, Otis Williams from the Temptations, the Commodores, Rick James, and lots of other notables. He even has an impressive collection of their framed gold and platinum records with personal inscriptions to him.

My cousin has owned some handsome cars during his lifetime that he's driven with the pride of a peacock. This inspired the road trip idea.

Scoopy's voice and wisdom punctuate *Rhythm Ride*'s narrative. As the story unfolded—as Scoopy's inflections and humor flung forward—my role was to listen and to serve as an instrument for crafting the account. The Groove's telling of this tale is meant to inspire any reader who's ready to explore a musical tradition that became the Sound of Young America.

Timeline

1929

- Berry Gordy, Jr., is born November 28 in Detroit, Michigan.

1953

- The 3-D Record Mart is opened by Berry Gordy.
- Berry and Thelma Coleman marry.

1955

- The 3-D Record Mart shuts down.
- Berry begins to work on the assembly line at Ford's Lincoln-Mercury plant.

1957

- Berry quits Ford and cowrites his first hit song, "Reet Petite."
- William "Smokey" Robinson and Berry meet and forge a friendship.

1959

- Berry's family agrees to loan him eight hundred dollars from their savings to start his record company.
- The Gordys purchase a house at 2648 West Grand Boulevard in Detroit, Michigan, as the headquarters for their start-up. The company's building is called Hitsville U.S.A.; the Motown record label is established.

1960

- "Money (That's What I Want)" is released and is Motown's first hit. It is written by Berry Gordy and Janie Bradford and sung by Barrett Strong.

- The Miracles' record "Shop Around" becomes Motown's first million-copy seller. It also becomes the company's first Top 10 hit.
- Motown signs on the Marvelettes and Mary Wells.
- Mary Wells records "Bye, Bye, Baby" on the Motown label.

1961

- The Elgins audition for Motown and are signed under the name the Temptations.
- Motown signs Steveland Morris, whose name is changed to Stevie Wonder.
- Motown's first number one song, "Please Mr. Postman," is recorded by the Marvelettes. It is written by Brian Holland, Freddie Gorman, Robert Bateman, William Garrett, and Georgia Dobbins.
- Motown signs Diane Ross and the Primettes. Berry renames them the Supremes.

1962

- Brian Holland, Eddie Holland, and Lamont Dozier form Holland-Dozier-Holland, known as H-D-H, and begin to work as a songwriting and music production team.
- The Miracles, Martha and the Vandellas, the Supremes, Mary Wells, Little Stevie Wonder, Marvin Gaye, the Contours, and the Marvelettes get on a bus to travel with the Motortown Revue, which leaves Detroit to tour the East Coast and the South.
- Mary Wells becomes Motown's first solo superstar with three Top 10 hits.
- Mary Wells appears on the *American Bandstand* television show, hosted by Dick Clark.

1963

- Martha and the Vandellas' "(Love Is Like a) Heat Wave," written by H-D-H, makes it to the number one spot of the *Billboard* R&B Singles chart.
- Marvin Gaye's "Hitch Hike" and Little Stevie Wonder's "Fingertips (Part 2)" become hits.
- Dr. Martin Luther King, Jr., delivers his landmark "I Have a Dream" speech in Washington, D.C., at the March on Washington. More than 250,000 people participate in the march, where they listen to speeches by several civil rights leaders. Berry records Motown's first album of speeches by Dr. Martin Luther King, Jr., called *The Great March to Freedom*.
- President John F. Kennedy is assassinated in Dallas, Texas.

1964

- Motown's Artist Development department is established. Maxine Powell and Cholly Atkins groom Motown's performers.
- The Supremes appear on *The Ed Sullivan Show*.
- "The Way You Do the Things You Do" is the Temptations' first Top 20 hit.
- The Civil Rights Act of 1964 is signed into law by President Lyndon Johnson.

1965

- "My Girl," written by Smokey Robinson and sung by the Temptations, becomes a number one hit.
- "I Can't Help Myself (Sugar Pie Honey Bunch)," sung by the Four Tops, and "Stop! In the Name of Love," sung by the Supremes, each score number one hits.

1966

- Norman Whitfield begins producing the Temptations.
- Motown signs Gladys Knight and the Pips.

1967

- Martha and the Vandellas record "Jimmy Mack."
- The Supremes become Diana Ross and the Supremes. The group's name changes to reflect Diana as the lead singer.
- The Detroit riots begin, becoming one of the worst riots in the history of the United States.

1968

- Berry moves Motown's headquarters from West Grand Boulevard to 2457 Woodward Avenue in downtown Detroit.
- Berry Gordy hires Suzanne de Passe as his executive assistant.
- The *TCB—Taking Care of Business: Diana Ross and the Supremes with the Temptations* television special, created by Berry, airs nationally.
- The Jackson brothers audition at Motown and are signed by the company. Berry establishes them under the name the Jackson 5.
- Martin Luther King, Jr., is assassinated at the Lorraine Motel in Memphis, Tennessee.

1969

- When the Jackson 5 perform at a club called the Daisy in Beverly Hills, they are introduced by Diana Ross.
- The Jackson 5 sing "I Want You Back," which becomes their first Top 40 hit.

1970

- Diana Ross leaves the Supremes for a solo career.
- The song "War" is released. It is written by Norman Whitfield and Barrett Strong and sung by Edwin Starr.

1971

- *What's Going On*, created by Marvin Gaye, becomes Motown's bestselling album.

1972

- Motown moves its headquarters from Detroit, Michigan, to Hollywood, California. The Hitsville U.S.A. office in Detroit continues on.
- Suzanne de Passe heads up Motown Productions and produces the acclaimed film titled *Lady Sings the Blues*, starring Diana Ross as Billie Holiday.
- Motown signs Lionel Richie and the Commodores.
- The last U.S. troops are withdrawn from Vietnam.

1973

- The Jackson 5 leave Motown.

1981

- Diana Ross leaves Motown for RCA Records.
- Suzanne de Passe becomes president of Motown Productions.

1982

- Lionel Richie begins a string of Top 10 hits for Motown, including a song titled "Truly."

1983

- The TV special *Motown 25: Yesterday, Today, Forever* airs on NBC.
- Martin Luther King Day becomes a federal holiday.

1985

- Berry's sister, Esther Gordy Edwards, opens the Motown Museum at the former Hitsville U.S.A. studio.

1988

- Berry is inducted into the Rock and Roll Hall of Fame.
- Berry sells several assets of the Motown company to MCA Records.

1994

- *To Be Loved: The Music, the Magic, the Memories of Motown—An Autobiography* by Berry Gordy is published.

1996

- Berry Gordy accepts a star on the Hollywood Walk of Fame from Mayor Johnny Grant.

1997

- Berry sells a portion of Motown to EMI.

1998

- ABC airs a television special called *Motown 40: The Music Is Forever.*

2013

- *Motown: The Musical* premieres on Broadway at the Lunt-Fontanne Theatre on April 14. Its script book was written by Berry Gordy and is based on Berry Gordy's autobiography, *To Be Loved: The Music, the Magic, the Memories of Motown—An Autobiography.*

Selected Discography

Now it's your turn to drive. To steer on your own. To travel back to the days when Berry Gordy's music ruled the airwaves. Here is a map to lead the way. A timeline that will put you on the road to Motown's music. This list includes many of the top-selling singles and some of the bestselling albums produced by Motown Records. Some we met on our trip. Others listed are here for you to discover on your own. What do you mean you don't have a driver's license? You don't need a license to listen, kid. Just sit back and let the music take you.

YEAR	SONG	PERFORMER(S)
1960	"Shop Around"	The Miracles
1961	"Please Mr. Postman"	The Marvelettes
1962	"Do You Love Me"	The Contours
	"Twistin' Postman"	The Marvelettes
	"The One Who Really Loves You"	Mary Wells
	"You Beat Me to the Punch"	Mary Wells

	"Two Lovers"	Mary Wells
	"Playboy"	The Marvelettes
	"Beechwood 4-5789"	The Marvelettes
	"Hitch Hike"	Marvin Gaye
	"You've Really Got a Hold on Me"	The Miracles
1963	"(Love Is Like a) Heat Wave"	Martha and the Vandellas
	"Pride and Joy"	Marvin Gaye
	"Fingertips (Part 2)"	Little Stevie Wonder
	"Quicksand"	Martha and the Vandellas
	"Can I Get a Witness"	Marvin Gaye
	The Great March to Freedom (album)	Rev. Martin Luther King, Jr. (speeches)
1964	"My Guy"	Mary Wells
	"Dancing in the Street"	Martha and the Vandellas
	"The Way You Do the Things You Do"	The Temptations
	"Baby I Need Your Loving"	The Four Tops
	"Where Did Our Love Go"	The Supremes
	"Baby Love"	The Supremes
	"Come See About Me"	The Supremes
	"How Sweet It Is (To Be Loved by You)"	Marvin Gaye
	"My Girl"	The Temptations
1965	"Nowhere to Run"	Martha and the Vandellas
	"Stop! In the Name of Love"	The Supremes
	"Back in My Arms Again"	The Supremes
	"I Can't Help Myself"	The Four Tops
	"Nothing but Heartaches"	The Supremes
	"I Hear a Symphony"	The Supremes

	"Shotgun"	Junior Walker and the All Stars
	"The Tracks of My Tears"	The Miracles
	"It's the Same Old Song"	The Four Tops
	"Ain't That Peculiar"	Marvin Gaye
	"My World Is Empty Without You"	The Supremes
1966	"Don't Mess with Bill"	The Marvelettes
	"Uptight (Everything's Alright)"	Stevie Wonder
	"Love Is Like an Itching in My Heart"	The Supremes
	"You Can't Hurry Love"	The Supremes
	"Reach Out I'll Be There"	The Four Tops
	"Ain't Too Proud to Beg"	The Temptations
	"I'm Ready for Love"	Martha and the Vandellas
	"You Keep Me Hangin' On"	The Supremes
	"Beauty Is Only Skin Deep"	The Temptations
	"(I Know) I'm Losing You"	The Temptations
	"What Becomes of the Brokenhearted"	Jimmy Ruffin
	"(I'm a) Road Runner"	Junior Walker and the All Stars
	"Standing in the Shadows of Love"	The Four Tops
	"Heaven Must Have Sent You"	The Elgins
1967	"Ain't No Mountain High Enough"	Marvin Gaye and Tammi Terrell
	"I Was Made to Love Her"	Stevie Wonder
	"Love Is Here and Now You're Gone"	The Supremes
	"I Second That Emotion"	Smokey Robinson and the Miracles
	"Jimmy Mack"	Martha and the Vandellas
	"Your Precious Love"	Marvin Gaye and Tammi Terrell
	"If I Could Build My Whole World Around You"	Marvin Gaye and Tammi Terrell

	"All I Need"	The Temptations
	"You're My Everything"	The Temptations
	"Bernadette"	The Four Tops
	"The Happening"	The Supremes
	"Reflections"	Diana Ross and the Supremes
	"I Heard It Through the Grapevine"	Gladys Knight and the Pips
	"I Wish It Would Rain"	The Temptations
1968	"Ain't Nothing Like the Real Thing"	Marvin Gaye and Tammi Terrell
	"For Once in My Life"	Stevie Wonder
	Free at Last (album)	Rev. Martin Luther King, Jr. (speeches)
	"You're All I Need to Get By"	Marvin Gaye and Tammi Terrell
	"Cloud Nine"	The Temptations
	"Love Child"	Diana Ross and the Supremes
	"I'm Gonna Make You Love Me"	Diana Ross and the Supremes and The Temptations
1969	"I'm Livin' in Shame"	Diana Ross and the Supremes
	"My Cherie Amour"	Stevie Wonder
	"Abraham, Martin and John"	Smokey Robinson and the Miracles
	"Friendship Train"	Gladys Knight and the Pips
	"I Can't Get Next to You"	The Temptations
	"Someday We'll Be Together"	Diana Ross and the Supremes
	"I Want You Back"	The Jackson 5
	"Psychedelic Shack"	The Temptations
1970	"ABC"	The Jackson 5
	"The Love You Save"	The Jackson 5
	"I'll Be There"	The Jackson 5

"War"	Edwin Starr
"Up the Ladder to the Roof"	The Supremes (without Diana Ross)
"The Tears of a Clown"	Smokey Robinson and the Miracles
"Ball of Confusion (That's What the World Is Today)"	The Temptations
"Signed, Sealed, Delivered, I'm Yours"	Stevie Wonder
"It's a Shame"	The Spinners
"Get Ready"	Rare Earth
"If I Were Your Woman"	Gladys Knight and the Pips
"Reach Out and Touch (Somebody's Hand)"	Diana Ross
"Stoned Love"	The Supremes

1971	"Stop the War Now"	Edwin Starr
	"Just My Imagination (Running Away with Me)"	The Temptations
	"What's Going On"	Marvin Gaye
	"Superstar (Remember How You Got Where You Are)"	The Temptations
	"Never Can Say Goodbye"	The Jackson 5
	"Got to Be There"	Michael Jackson

1972	"Rockin' Robin"	Michael Jackson
	"Ben"	Michael Jackson
	"Superstition"	Stevie Wonder
	"Papa Was a Rollin' Stone"	The Temptations

| 1973 | "Let's Get It On" | Marvin Gaye |
| | "You Are the Sunshine of My Life" | Stevie Wonder |

	"Neither One of Us (Wants to Be the First to Say Goodbye)"	Gladys Knight and the Pips
	"Keep On Truckin' (Part 1)"	Eddie Kendricks
	"Living for the City"	Stevie Wonder
	"Boogie Down"	Eddie Kendricks
1974	"Don't You Worry 'Bout a Thing"	Stevie Wonder
	"Boogie On Reggae Woman"	Stevie Wonder
	"Machine Gun"	The Commodores
1975	"Love Machine (Part 1)"	The Miracles (without Smokey Robinson)
	"Theme from *Mahogany* (Do You Know Where You're Going To)"	Diana Ross
1976	"Sweet Love"	The Commodores
	"Just to Be Close to You"	The Commodores
	"I Wish"	Stevie Wonder
	"Love Hangover"	Diana Ross
1977	"Sir Duke"	Stevie Wonder
	"Easy"	The Commodores
	"Brick House"	The Commodores
1978	"Three Times a Lady"	The Commodores
1979	"Sail On"	The Commodores
	"Still"	The Commodores
	"Cruisin'"	Smokey Robinson
1980	"Upside Down"	Diana Ross
	"I'm Coming Out"	Diana Ross
	"Master Blaster (Jammin')"	Stevie Wonder
	"It's My Turn"	Diana Ross
	"I Need Your Lovin'"	Teena Marie
1981	"Being with You"	Smokey Robinson

	"Happy Birthday"	Stevie Wonder
	"Super Freak"	Rick James
	"Lady (You Bring Me Up)"	The Commodores
	"That Girl"	Stevie Wonder
1982	"Truly"	Lionel Richie
1983	"You Are"	Lionel Richie
	"My Love"	Lionel Richie
	"All Night Long (All Night)"	Lionel Richie
	"Running with the Night"	Lionel Richie
1984	"Hello"	Lionel Richie
	"Stuck on You"	Lionel Richie
	"Penny Lover"	Lionel Richie
	"I Just Called to Say I Love You"	Stevie Wonder
	"Treat Her Like a Lady"	The Temptations
1985	"Nightshift"	The Commodores (without Lionel Richie)
	"In My House"	Mary Jane Girls
	"Part-Time Lover"	Stevie Wonder
	"Say You, Say Me"	Lionel Richie
	"Rhythm of the Night"	DeBarge
1986	"Dancing on the Ceiling"	Lionel Richie
	"Who's Johnny"	El DeBarge
	"Love Will Conquer All"	Lionel Richie
	"Ballerina Girl"	Lionel Richie
1987	"Respect Yourself"	Bruce Willis
	"Just to See Her"	Smokey Robinson
	"One Heartbeat"	Smokey Robinson
	"Se La"	Lionel Richie
1988	"Do You Love Me" (re-release)	The Contours

On Screen

Stars seem far away when you're looking at them high in the sky. If you want to see some of Motown's brightest up close, watch these television programs and movies that were produced by Berry Gordy's Motown Productions.

Television

1968   *TCB—Taking Care of Business: Diana Ross and the Supremes with the Temptations* (special)

1969   *GIT (Get It Together) on Broadway* (special, starring Diana Ross and the Supremes and the Temptations)

1971   *Diana!* (special, starring Diana Ross and introducing the Jackson 5)

1971   *Goin' Back to Indiana* (special, starring the Jackson 5)

1977   *Scott Joplin* (movie)

1983   *Motown 25: Yesterday, Today, Forever* (special)

1985   *Motown Returns to the Apollo* (special)

1985   *The Motown Revue* (series, hosted by Smokey Robinson)

1986   *Motown on Showtime* (series)

Motion Pictures

1972   *Lady Sings the Blues*

1975   *Mahogany*

1976   *The Bingo Long Traveling All-Stars & Motor Kings*

1978   *Almost Summer*

1978   *Thank God, It's Friday*

1978   *The Wiz*

1985   *The Last Dragon*

Source Notes

Frontispiece quotations:

Berry Gordy quote: Motown Museum website home page www.motownmuseum.org

Smokey Robinson quote: *Christianity Today* article by Andy Argyrakis, June 14, 2004.

Dick Clark quote: *Motown 25: Yesterday, Today, Forever* television special, NBC.

Marvin Gaye quote: *Motown 25: Yesterday, Today, Forever* television special, NBC.

Joe Hunter quote: *Standing in the Shadows of Motown* documentary, Artisan Entertainment, 2002.

A Greeting from the Groove

Inspired by interviews with James K. Snowden, Jr., December 2013–February 2014.

Motor City

Accounts of Berry Gordy's childhood and family life are derived from several sources, including: *To Be Loved: The Music, the Magic, the Memories of Motown—An Autobiography* by Berry Gordy, chapters 1-6; "Berry Gordy's Childhood Lesson on Race," *Master Class*, Oprah Winfrey Network, accompanying narrative published on June 16, 2013; The Motown Historical Museum website: www.motownmuseum.org/; Famous Entrepreneurs website: www.famous-entrepreneurs.com/berry-gordy

Information about the Ford Motor Company's history and hiring practices is found on the Ford Motor Company website: www.corporate.ford.com/company/history.html

"No gag too big, no laugh too small . . .": *The History of Motown* by Virginia Aronson, page 13 and "Facts on File History Database Center," Chapter 1, *The History of Motown*, African-American Achievers, page 2.

Handsome Dazzler

A description of Berry Gordy's shoeshine stand is found in: Aronson, *The History of Motown*, 13; Gordy, *To Be Loved: The Music, the Magic, the Memories of Motown—An Autobiography*, 38, 39.

Details about Berry Gordy's newspaper sales of the *Michigan Chronicle* are found in: *The Pittsburgh Courier*, November 18, 2013.

A description of Berry Gordy's career as a boxer is found in: Aronson, *The History of Motown*, 13–14; Gordy, *To Be Loved: The Music, the Magic, the Memories of Motown—An Autobiography*, 43–49.

Got a Job

Information about The 3-D Record Mart is described in: Aronson, *The History of Motown*, 15–16; Berry Gordy's salary at Ford is found on page 16.

Berry Gordy's recollection of how he and Smokey Robinson met is recounted in: Gordy, *To Be Loved: The Music, the Magic, the Memories of Motown—An Autobiography*, 90–94; and is depicted in: *Motown: The Musical*, which appeared at the Lunt-Fontanne Theatre, New York, NY, script book by Berry Gordy.

Information about Berry Gordy's "Got a Job" royalties is found in: Aronson, *The History of Motown*, 21.

Dreaming Big for Eight Hundred Dollars

The story about Berry Gordy borrowing money from his family is found in: Gordy, *To Be Loved: The Music, the Magic, the Memories of Motown—An Autobiography*, 104–108; the Motown Historical Museum website: www.motownmuseum.org

Hitsville U.S.A. is described in detail in the online article: Robert Dennis, "Our Motown Heritage (Part 24)": www.recordingeq.com/2006motown/06motown24.html

Its creation is also depicted in *Motown: The Musical*, which appeared at the Lunt-Fontanne Theatre, New York, NY.

The Motown Family

"If you only had a dollar in your pocket . . ." Berry Gordy interview as part of "Oprah's Master Class," Season 3, Episode 307, aired June 16, 2013.

Descriptions of Hitsville quality-control meetings found in: Gordy, *To Be Loved: The Music, the Magic, the Memories of Motown—An Autobiography*, 104–108; The Motown Historical Museum: www.motownmuseum.org

My Mama Told Me

Recounting of Berry waking Smokey Robinson at three o'clock in the morning found in: Gordy, *To Be Loved: The Music, the Magic, the Memories of Motown—An Autobiography*, 142–144.

Creation of the song "Money (That's What I Want)" is described in: Aronson, *The History of Motown*, 28. Information about the song is also found on the Soul Walking website: Berry Gordy page: http://www.soulwalking.co.uk/Berry%20Gordy.html

Factory Rhythm

Recounting of Berry Gordy's interactions with Mary Wells and the creation of "My Guy" appear in: Gordy, *To Be Loved: The Music, the Magic, the Memories of Motown—An Autobiography*, 138–140.

Accounts of the creation of "Please Mr. Postman" are found in several sources, including: The "Song Facts" website: www.songfacts.com/detail.php?id=25; The Rock and Roll Hall of Fame website: www.rockhall.com/inductees/nominees/the-marvelettes/; Aronson, *The History of Motown*, 30.

The C Circuit

Accounts of the chitlin circuit are drawn from: National Public Radio's "The Origin (and Hot Stank) of the Chitlin' Circuit" by Tanya Ballard Brown, February 16, 2014, 7:00 p.m.

Accounts of the social unrest during the Motortown Revue are cited in "An Invitation Across the Nation" article "Motortown Revue of 1962—Into the Dismal Heart of Jim Crow": www.invitationacrossthenation.com/part2

Miss Manners

Recollections of Maxine Powell's work with Motown performers are taken from: "Remembering the Woman Who Gave Motown Its Charm," NPR interview with Maxine Powell by Gene Demby, October 15, 2013; *All Things Considered* interview with Rebecca Roberts, 2009.

Additional Maxine Powell details found in: Gordy, *To Be Loved: The Music, the Magic, the Memories of Motown—An Autobiography,* 176, 216; Aronson, *The History of Motown,* 39, 59; and Jack Ryan, *Recollections, the Detroit Years: The Motown Sound by the People Who Made It,* 2–5.

Cholly's Moves

Memories of Cholly Atkins's work with Motown talent is cited in: Ryan, *Recollections, the Detroit Years: The Motown Sound by the People Who Made It,* 2–5, and can be found on: the Motown Historical Museum tour and website: www.motownmuseum.org

Dancing in the Street

Mary Wells's not showing up to a recording session and Martha Reeves's stepping in to sing "(Love Is Like a) Heat Wave" is described in: Aronson, *The History of Motown,* 42.

Details about the creation of "Dancing in the Street" are found in: Gordy, *To Be Loved: The Music, the Magic, the Memories of Motown—An Autobiography,* 202, 203.

Additional source material found in: Suzanne E. Smith, *Dancing in the Street: Motown and the Cultural Politics of Detroit*; Kingsley Abbott, ed., *Calling Out Around the World: A Motown Reader*.

Wonder Kid

Information about Berry Gordy's breakfast being interrupted is found in: Gordy, *To Be Loved: The Music, the Magic, the Memories of Motown—An Autobiography*, 148.

Accounts of Maxine Powell's work with Stevie Wonder are taken from: "Remembering the Woman Who Gave Motown Its Charm," NPR interview with Maxine Powell by Gene Demby, October 15, 2013; *All Things Considered* interview with Rebecca Roberts, 2009.

Recollections of discovering and signing Stevie Wonder are taken from: PBS Berry Gordy interview with Tavis Smiley, January 8, 2009. www.pbs.org/kcet/tavissmiley /archive/200901/20090109

The "Song Facts" website describes the creation of "Fingertips"/"Fingertips 2": www .songfacts.com/detail.php?id=436/; Quincy Troupe, *Little Stevie Wonder*. The live concert at which the song was performed can also be viewed on YouTube.

The Funk Brothers

Accounts about the Funk Brothers are drawn from the documentary film: *Standing in the Shadows of Motown*, Artisan Entertainment, 2002.

Additional information is found in: Don Waller, *The Motown Story*, 154–167.

Ugly Sightseeing

Civil rights accounts found in: Phillip Hoose, *Claudette Colvin: Twice Toward Justice*, Melanie Kroupa Books, Farrar Straus Giroux, New York, 2009; *Eyes on the Prize: America's Civil Rights Movement* by Henry Hampton Blackside, Inc. DVD. PBS Video, 2006.

Information about *The Great March to Freedom* album was found at: "Motown: The Truth Is a Hit" exhibition, Schomburg Center for Research in Black Culture.

Sunshine on a Cloudy Day

Facts about the beginnings of Motown's international distribution with EMI appear in: Brett Lashua, Karl Spracklen, Stephen Wagg, eds., *Sounds and the City: Popular Music, Place and Globalization*, 120.

Information about the Four Tops is found in several sources, including: Gordy, *To Be Loved: The Music, the Magic, the Memories of Motown—An Autobiography*; The Motown Historical Museum website: www.motownmuseum.org; *Motown: The Musical* at the Lunt-Fontanne Theatre, New York, NY; Ryan, *Recollections, the Detroit Years: The Motown Sound by the People Who Made It*.

Berry Gordy quote "Communication breeds understanding . . ." is found in the online magazine article: "Motown the Musical: Berry Gordy in His Own Words," May 30, 2014: magazine.shnsf.com/index.php/stories/motown-the-musical-berry-gordy-in-his-own-words/

Details about Cholly's work with the Temptations are found in: Ryan, *Recollections, the Detroit Years: The Motown Sound by the People Who Made It*, 2–4.

Particulars of Bobby Rogers and Smokey Robinson working together are recounted in: Gordy, *To Be Loved: The Music, the Magic, the Memories of Motown—An Autobiography*, 222, 223.

The Sound of Young America

Information about "Get Ready" is found in several sources, including: Gordy, *To Be Loved: The Music, the Magic, the Memories of Motown—An Autobiography*; The Motown Historical Museum website: www.motownmuseum.org; *Motown: The Musical* at the Lunt-Fontanne Theatre, New York, NY; Ryan, *Recollections, the Detroit Years: The Motown Sound by the People Who Made It*.

Information about Norman Whitfield and his creation of "I Heard It Through the Grapevine" is described in: Gordy, *To Be Loved: The Music, the Magic, the Memories of Motown—An Autobiography*, 272, 273.

Singing Supreme

Information about the Supremes and their discovery is depicted in: *Motown: The Musical* at the Lunt-Fontanne Theatre, New York, NY; Aronson, *The History of Motown*, 39, 54, 55, 57–59; *Motown 25: Yesterday, Today, Forever*, television special.

Recollections of Maxine Powell's grooming of the Supremes is taken from: "Remembering the Woman Who Gave Motown Its Charm," NPR interview with Maxine Powell, by Gene Demby, October 15, 2013; All Things Considered interview with Rebecca Roberts, 2009.

Family Drama

Motown family strife and the Motown UK Tour is cited in: Aronson, *The History of Motown*, 39, 59, 61, 63–65.

Motown's family struggles are referenced in: *This Day in History Mar 25, 1983:* "The Motown 'family' stages a bittersweet reunion performance." www.history.com/this-day-in-history/the-motown-family-stages-a-bittersweet-reunion-performance

What's Going On

Creation of the song "Abraham, Martin and John" is described in: "Behind the Song: 'Abraham, Martin and John'" by David Freeland, *American Songwriter*, December 2, 2009.

The unveiling of the song "War" and its progression are described in: *Mojo* magazine, February 2009; *Motown: The Musical* at the Lunt-Fontanne Theatre, New York, NY.

Detailed accounts of the Detroit riots appear in the following sources: *This Day in History Jul 23, 1967:* "The 12th Street riot." www.history.com/this-day-in-history/the-12th-street-riot; BlackPast.org: Detroit Race Riots, 1967: www.blackpast.org/aah/detroit-race-riot-1967

Recollections of Marvin Gaye and his brother Frankie are cited throughout: Frankie Gaye with Fred Basten, *Marvin Gaye, My Brother.*

Marvin Gaye's call to Berry Gordy in the Bahamas, Marvin presenting Berry with "What Going On," and the song's early development are recounted in: Gordy, *To Be Loved: The Music, the Magic, the Memories of Motown—An Autobiography*, 302, 303; and depicted in: *Motown: The Musical* at the Lunt-Fontanne Theatre, New York, NY.

The influences of Harry Balk and Barney Ales on the success of "What's Going On" can be found on: Harry Balk Lifetime Achievement Award, Detroit Music Awards, published online, October 11, 2013. www.youtube.com/watch?v=8XeIY_cnwZw

Notable citations of "What's Going On" are in: "The 500 Greatest Albums of All Time." *Rolling Stone* magazine. Wenner Media Specials, 2012.

TCB, ABC, 1-2-3-4-5

Motown's move to LA is described in: Gordy, *To Be Loved: The Music, the Magic, the Memories of Motown—An Autobiography*, chapters 10 and 11.

The *TCB* special is rendered on: *TCB—Taking Care of Business: Diana Ross and the Supremes and the Temptations*, 1968, produced by the Video Beat.

The hiring of Suzanne de Passe is described in: Gordy, *To Be Loved: The Music, the Magic, the Memories of Motown—An Autobiography*, 260, 261.

Recollections of discovering and signing Michael Jackson are taken from: PBS Berry Gordy interview with Tavis Smiley, January 8, 2009. www.youtube.com/watch?v=VWQKdVpS6Lk

Suzanne de Passe's work with the Jackson 5 is recalled in: "Suzanne De Passe remembers the Jackson 5," an interview that appears on The Official Black List YouTube Page, June 26, 2009. www.youtube.com/watch?v=jVVMEOh3qpI

Details about the Jackson 5 are depicted in: *The Jacksons: An American Dream* miniseries, originally broadcast on November 15 through November 18, 1992, on ABC television.

New Directions

Information about Diana Ross's career is described throughout: Diana Ross, *Secrets of a Sparrow*, a memoir.

Stevie Wonder's activism is described in: Joel from Fredericksburg, "Musician Hero: Stevie Wonder"; Troupe, *Little Stevie Wonder.*

Characterizations of Lionel Richie, DeBarge, Rick James, and Teena Marie are depicted in: *Motown: The Musical* at the Lunt-Fontanne Theatre, New York, NY.

The Groove Goes On

Berry Gordy and other Motown family members' induction into the Rock and Roll Hall of Fame is described on the Michigan Rock and Roll Legends website: www.michiganrockandrolllegends.com/mrrl-hall-of-fame/103-berry-gordy-jr

Berry Gordy's Hollywood Walk of Fame Star is cited in: Graham Betts, *Motown Encyclopedia*; David Edwards and Mike Callahan, *The Motown Story*, August 8, 2012. www.bsnpubs.com/motown/gordystory.html; Aronson, *The History of Motown*, 92.

Details about the sale of Motown are taken from: James Bates, "Berry Gordy Sells Motown Records for $61 Million," *Los Angeles Times*, June 29, 1988.

Information about the sales of Motown's publishing rights can be found in: Andrew Ross Sorkin, "Berry Gordy Sells EMI a Stake in Catalogue of Motown Songs," the *New York Times*, July 2, 1997.

The White House Motown tribute is described in: Matthew Perpetua, "Obama Celebrates Motown Records at the White House," February 25, 2011, www.rollingstone.com/music/news/obama-celebrates-motown-records-at-the-white-house-20110225

For Further Enjoyment

Rhythm Ride is one of many trips to Motown. This book's road map was created by consulting several books, magazines, DVDs, and websites. Here is a list of many of them, and some additional sources you may find interesting.

Books, Magazines, and DVDs

Abbott, Kingsley, ed. *Calling Out Around the World: A Motown Reader*. London: Helter Skelter Publishing, 2001.

Adelman, Bob, and Charles Johnson. *Mine Eyes Have Seen: Bearing Witness to the Struggle for Civil Rights*. New York: Time Inc. Home Entertainment Books, 2007.

Altman, Susan. *Extraordinary African-Americans*. New York: Children's Press, 2001.

Aronson, Virginia. *The History of Motown*. Philadelphia: Chelsea House Publishers, 2001.

Beller, Miles. "Making Motown's Movies." *Harper's Bazaar*, September 1985.

Betts, Graham. *Motown Encyclopedia*. Smashwords, June 2014.

Bianco, David. *Heat Wave: The Motown Fact Book*. Ann Arbor, MI: Pierian Press, 1988.

Bolden, Tonya. *MLK—Journey of a King*. New York: Harry N. Abrams, Inc., 2007.

Branch, Taylor. *Parting the Waters: America in the King Years 1954–63*. New York: Simon & Schuster Paperbacks, 1988.

"Brotherhood Crusade Salutes Motown's Berry Gordy." *Jet*, January 30, 1989.

Carson, Clayborne, David J. Garrow, Gerald Gill, Vincent Harding, and Darlene Clark Hine. *The Eyes on the Prize Civil Rights Reader*. New York: Viking Penguin, 1991.

Carson, Clayborne, and Kris Shepard. *A Call to Conscience: The Landmark Speeches of Dr. Martin Luther King, Jr.* New York: Warner Books, Inc., 2001.

Castro, Janice. "Hitsville Goes Hollywood." *Time*, January 30, 1989.

Cox, Ted. *The Temptations*. Philadelphia: Chelsea House Publishers, 1997.

Darden, Bob. *People Get Ready: A New History of Black Gospel Music*. New York: Continuum, 2004.

DeCurtis, Anthony, and James Henke, eds. *The Rolling Stone Illustrated History of Rock and Roll*. New York: Random House, 1992.

Early, Gerald. *One Nation Under a Groove: Motown and American Culture*. Hopewell, N.J.: Ecco Press, 1995.

Fong-Torres, Ben. *The Motown Album*. New York: St. Martin's Press, 1990.

Gaye, Frankie, with Fred Basten. *Marvin Gaye, My Brother*. San Francisco: Backbeat Books, 2003.

George, Nelson. *Where Did Our Love Go? The Rise and Fall of the Motown Sound*. New York: St. Martin's Press, 1985.

Gordy, Berry. *To Be Loved: The Music, the Magic, the Memories of Motown*. New York: Warner Books, 1994.

Hampton, Henry. *Eyes on the Prize: America's Civil Rights Movement*. Blackside, Inc. DVD. PBS Video, 2006.

Hardy, James Earl. *Boyz II Men*. Philadelphia: Chelsea House Publishers, 1996.

Horwich, Richard, ed. *Michael Jackson*. New York: Gallery Books, 1984.

King, Martin Luther, Jr. *I Have a Dream*. New York: Scholastic Press, 1997.

"MCA/Boston Ventures Buy Motown for $61 Million." *Jet*, July 18, 1988.

Morse, David. *Motown*. New York: Collier Books, 1971.

Mussari, Mark. *Suzanne de Passe: Motown's Boss Lady*. Ada, OK: Garrett Educational Corporation, 1991.

Pareles, Jon, and Patricia Romanowski, eds. *The Rolling Stone Encyclopedia of Rock and Roll*. New York: Rolling Stone Press/Summit Books, 1983.

Powell, Maxine, and Julie Greenwalt. "Rock 'n' Role Model." *People Weekly*, October 13, 1986.

Ritz, David. *Divided Soul: The Life of Marvin Gaye*. New York: McGraw-Hill, 1991.

Ritz, David. "Soul Serenade." *TV Guide*, February 14, 1998.

Ryan, Jack. *Recollections, the Detroit Years: The Motown Sound by the People Who Made It*. Whitmore Lake, MI: Glendower Media, LLC, 2012.

Singleton, Raynoma Gordy. *Berry, Me, and Motown: The Untold Story*. Chicago: Contemporary Books, 1991.

Smith, Suzanne E. *Dancing in the Street: Motown and the Cultural Politics of Detroit*. Cambridge, MA: Harvard University Press, 1999.

Taraborrelli, J. Randy. *Call Her Miss Ross*. Secaucus, N.J.: Carol Publishing Group, 1989.

"The 500 Greatest Albums of All Time." *Rolling Stone* magazine. Wenner Media Specials, 2012.

Waller, Don. *The Motown Story*. New York: Charles Scriber's Sons, 1985.

Whitall, Susan. *Women of Motown: An Oral History*. New York: Harper's, 1998.

Whitburn, Joel. *The Billboard Book of Top 40 Hits*, 6th edition. New York: Billboard Books, 1996.

Websites

Ford Motor Company

corporate.ford.com/our-company/heritage

The Motown Record Company

www.motown.com

The Motown Museum

www.motownmuseum.org

Rock and Roll Hall of Fame and Museum

www.rockhall.com

Theatrical Productions

Motown: The Musical: script book by Berry Gordy, based on Berry Gordy's *To Be Loved: The Music, the Magic, the Memories of Motown—An Autobiography.*

Standing in the Shadows of Motown documentary, Artisan Entertainment, 2002. Director: Paul Justman. Writers: Walter Dallas (Narration), Ntozake Shange (Narration).

Acknowledgments

A Rhythm Ride requires many friends and helpers to navigate the road, and to offer direction and guidance. Special thanks to the following individuals and institutions for their research assistance, and for staying the course as our journey unfolded: Coraleen Rawls, Chief Archivist, Motown Museum and Curator of "Motown: The Truth Is a Hit" exhibition, Schomburg Center for Research in Black Culture, The New York Public Library, New York, NY, February 1–July 26, 2014. The exhibition was presented by Northern Trust, in partnership with Schomburg Center for Research in Black Culture. Antonio Dandridge from Detroit's Motown Museum; Payal Doshi, research coordinator; many patient librarians from the Schomburg Center for Research in Black Culture.

Thank you, Steve Diamond, Beth Potter, and Claire Dorsett for your tireless work in helping to wrangle so many compelling photographs.

Gratitude goes to my editor, Katherine Jacobs, for her keen editorial eye and enthusiasm. Thank you, Senior Creative Director Anne Diebel, for your friendship, humor, and insight. To my agent, Rebecca Sherman, thank you for keeping me on the right road.

To my cousin, James K. Snowden, Jr., I am spilling over with thankfulness for bringing this story to life and for making the journey so much fun. To Mom and Dad, and to Jerry and Gloria, thank you for spinning all that vinyl, and for teaching me to croon. To Chloe and Dobbin, you make my heart sing. And to Brian, how sweet it is to be loved by you.

Photo Credits

Page ii: The Tony Spina Collection, Walter P. Reuther Library, Archives of Labor and Urban Affairs, Wayne State University; vi, viii: Michael Ochs Archives/Getty Images; 4: Authenticated News/Archive Photos/Getty Images; 6: Underwood Archives/Archive Photos/Getty Images; 11: Bettmann/Corbis; 12: Hulton-Deutsch Collection/Corbis; 17, 18, 25: Michael Ochs Archives/Getty Images; 29: Steve Kagan/The *LIFE* Images Collection/Getty Images; 34: CA/Redferns/Getty Images; 36: Michael Ochs Archives/Getty Images; 38: David Redfern/Redferns/Getty Images; 40, 42: Michael Ochs Archives/Getty Images; 44: Gilles Petard/Redferns/Getty Images; 46: *New York Daily News* Archive/*New York Daily News*/Getty Images; 50, 52: Michael Ochs Archives/Getty Images; 54: Associated Press/Tony Ding; 56, 60: Michael Ochs Archives/Getty Images; 62: GAB Archive/Redferns/Getty Images; 66: Michael Ochs Archives/Getty Images; 69, 71: GAB Archive/Redferns/Getty Images; 76: AP/AP/Corbis; 80, 83, 85, 86: Michael Ochs Archives/Getty Images; 88: Courtesy of the E. Azalia Hackley Collection of African Americans in the Performing Arts, Detroit Public Library; 91, 94: GAB Archive/Redferns/Getty Images; 96: Bettmann/Corbis; 100: Echoes/Redferns/Getty Images; 102: Mondadori/Getty Images; 105: Charlie Gillett Collection/Redferns/Getty Images; 110: Jim Britt/Michael Ochs Archives/Getty Images; 115, 117, 119, 122: Michael Ochs Archives/Getty Images; 124: NBC/NBCUniversal/Getty Images; 125: Rob Verhorst/Redferns/Getty Images; 129: Michael Stewart/WireImage/Getty Images; 130: Courtesy of the author; 139: Frank Dandridge/*Look* magazine/King Rose Archives.

Index

Numbers in *italic* indicate pages with illustrations

"ABC," 119–20
"Abraham, Martin and John," 108
Academy Awards, 122
African Americans, 5, 7, 18, 33, 36, 46, 131
    company ownership by, 122, 130
    culture of, 10, 45
    at Ford, *6*
    hate crimes against, 75–77, 104–7
    racial pride of, 87, 107
"Ain't Too Proud to Beg," 88–89
"All I Could Do Was Cry," 17
American Bandstand, 119, 134
Anderson, Katherine, 40
Anna Records, 19
Apollo Theater, 45, *46*, 56
A&R department, 63
Artist Development division, 50–51, 54, 55, 135
assassinations, 107, 108, 135, 136
Atkins, Cholly, *56*, 135
    choreography of, 55, 61, 82, *91*
    singing pantomime of, 57–58, *96*

"Baby I Need Your Loving," 81–82
Ballard, Florence, *94*, 95, 101
Bateman, Robert, 41, 134
Benjamin, Benny, *71*, 88
Benson, Obie, *80*, 81–82
Billboard, 35, 38, 41, 61, 64, 69, 82, 89, 97, 109, 111, 118, 135
Black Miss America pageant, 118
Blanding, Tanya, 106
Bradford, Janie, 33, 133
Brown, James, 117
Bryant, Elbridge ("Al"), 82, 84
"Bye, Bye, Baby," 134

the *C* circuit, 47
choreography, 55, *56*, 57–58, 61, 82, *91*, *96*, 97
Civil Rights Act (1964), 135
Clark, Chris, 122
Coleman, Thelma, 15, 16, 133
Collins, Addie Mae, 76, *77*
Colvin, Claudette, 75–76

The Commodores, 125, 132, 137
The Contours, 45, 57, 70, 101, 134
Cowart, Juanita, 40
Crosby, Hank, *71*

"Dancing in the Street," 64, 87, 128
Davis, Billy, *44*
Davis, Gwen, *130*
Davis, Phil, *130*
Day, Doris, *12*
de Passe, Suzanne, 116, 118, 122, 136, 137
DeBarge, 125
deejays, 44, 131
Detroit, *4*, 5, 8, 27, 28, 81
    Motown influence on, 74
    post-riot, war, 113–14
Detroit riots, *102*, 103, 105
    death toll, 106
    police raid beginning, 104, 136
Detroit's 20 Grand, 39, 90
Diana Ross and the Supremes, *96*, 99, *100*, 128, 134
    breakup, 121
    discovery, *94*, 95, 97–98
    number one hits by, 98, 135
    on *TCB*, 114, *115*, 136
disco, 125–26
Dobbins, Georgia, 40, 41, 134
doo-wop, 13, 61
Dozier, Lamont, *62*, 63, 81, 134

The Ed Sullivan Show, 135
Edwards, Dennis, 101
The Elgins. *See* The Temptations
EMI Music Publishing, 80, 128, 138

Fakir, Abdul ("Duke"), *80*, 81–82
fashion, 106–7
"Fingertips," 67–68, *69*, 135
Ford Motor Co., 5, *6*, 7, 15–16, 26, 33, 133
The Four Tops, *56*, *80*, 92, 123, 135
    H-D-H and, 81–82
    international success of, 99

Fox Theatre, *105*
Franklin, Melvin, 82, *83*
Free at Last, 107
Funk Brothers, *71*, 72, 88, 94, 112
Fuqua, Harvey, *44*

Garrett, William, 41, 134
Gaye, Frankie, 109
Gaye, Marvin, *44*, 45, 59, 63–64, 89–90, 91, 92, 101,
      134, 135, 137
    leaving Motown, 123
    stage presence of, *50, 52*
    war protest music of, 109, *110,* 111–12
Gladys Knight and the Pips, 89–90, *91*, 123, 128, 135
Gordy, Anna, 7, 17, 45, 51
Gordy, Berry, Jr., 2, 5, 13, 14, 22, 23, 24, *29*, 101
    Artist Development and, 50–51
    boxing career of, 10–11
    business model of, 26–27, 30–32, 33
    conflict with Gaye, M., 110–11
    early life of, 7–9, 15, 16, 133
    echo effect by, 74
    on equality, 79–80
    at Ford, 15–16, 33, 133
    The Great March to Freedom of, 77–78, 135
    Hitsville U.S.A. founded by, 25
    honors, 128, 138
    international appeal of, 100
    in Korean War, 12
    The Marvelettes discovered by, 40–41
    and Robinson, S., *129,* 133
    Ross discovered by, 94–95, 98
    Ross romance with, 121, *122*
    "Shop Around" beginnings with, 34–36
    as songwriter, 12, *17,* 18, 19, 133
    on touring, 43–44
    Wonder discovered by, 65–67
Gordy, Berry, Sr., 7
Gordy, Bertha, 7
Gordy, Esther, 24, 26, 138
Gordy, Fuller, 7, 27
Gordy, George, 7, 27
Gordy, Gwen, 7, 16, 17, 19–20, 51
Gordy, Loucye, 7, 26
Gordy, Robert, 7, 27
Gordy Print Shop, 7, 12, 13
Gordy Strip, 13
Gorman, Freddie, 134
gospel style, 60, 61, 74, 90

"Got a Job," 21, 29
The Great March to Freedom, 77–78, 107, 135
Greatest Hits (the Temptations Album), 89, 91
Guest, William, 89

Harlem, NY, 45–46, 88
hate crimes, 75–77, 104–7
H-D-H, *62*, 63, 81–82, 89, 95, 97, 123, 128, 134, 135
"Heat Wave," 60–61, 63
"Hitch Hike," 59, 135
Hitsville U.S.A., 30, 35
    ending of, 126, 127
    location of, 25, 28, 38, 133
    museum of, 128, 138
    performers, *29*
Holiday, Billie, 17, 122, 137
Holland, Brian, 41, *62*, 63, 81, 134
Holland, Eddie, *62*, 63, 81, 134
Holler, Dick, 108
Hollywood, 114–15, 121, 124, 136, 137
Hollywood Walk of Fame, 128
Horton, Gladys, 40
Hunter, Ivy Jo, 63
Hunter, Joe, *71*

"I Can't Help Myself (Sugar Pie Honey Bunch)," 82,
    135
"I Got the Feelin'," 116–17
"I Heard It Through the Grapevine," 89–91
"I Want You Back," 118, 136
international success, 80–81, 99–100

Jackson, Jackie, 116, *117*
Jackson, Jermaine, 116, *117,* 123
Jackson, Marlon, 116, *117*
Jackson, Michael, 116, *117,* 120
    albums, 123
    Grammy Award, *124*
Jackson, Randy, 123
Jackson, Tito, 116, *117*
The Jackson 5, 132, 136
    leaving Motown, changing name, 116, *117,* 123, 137
    marketing and, *119*
    television shows and, 118–20
The Jackson 5ive, 120
Jamerson, James, *71*
James, Etta, 17, 18
James, Rick, 125, 126, 132
Jim Crow Laws. *See* segregation laws

"Jimmy Mack," *105*, 136
Johnson, Lyndon B., 135

Kendricks, Eddie, 82, *83*
Kennedy, John F., 107, 108, 135
Kennedy, Robert F., 107
King, Martin Luther, Jr., 108
    assassination, 107, 136
    holiday, 124–25
    speeches, 77–78, 107, 110, 135
King, Maurice, *44*
Knight, Gladys. *See* Gladys Knight and the Pips
Knight, Merald ("Bubba"), 89
Korean War, 12

Lady Sings the Blues, 122, 137
Lincoln, Abraham, 108
Louis, Joe, 10, *11*

March on Washington, 77, 135
Marie, Teena, 125
Martha and the Vandellas, 45, *60*, 70, *86*, 87, 92,
    134, 136
    Billboard hits of, 61, 64, 135
    international success of, 99
    leaving Motown, 101, 123
Martin, Barbara, *94*, 95
Martin Luther King Day, 124, 125, 137
The Marvelettes, *40*, 41, *42*, 43, 45, 49, 70, 80, 92, 134
The Matadors, 20–21
MCA Records, 127, 138
McNair, Denise, 76, *77*
The Miracles, 21, 29, *36*, 38, *44*, 65, 70, 83, 134. *See also*
    The Matadors
    first Motown hit by, 35, 133
    international success of, 99
"Money (That's What I Want)," 33–34, 133
Moore, Warren ("Pete"), 21, *34*
Morris, Steveland. *See* Wonder, Stevie
Moses, Larry, 68–69
Motor City. *See* Detroit
Motortown Revue, *42*, 43, 49
    international tour, 100
    prejudice during, 46–47
    ten-week tour, 45–48, 134
Motown, 74. *See also* Hitsville U.S.A.
    Artist Development division, 50–51, 54, 55, 135
    artists leaving, 101, 116–17, 123, 136, 137
    assembly-line philosophy of, 26, 30, 31, 33, 38

assets sold, 80, 127–28, 138
beginnings of, 27, 133
code of ethics, 81
disco and, 125–26
family feeling of, 28–29
first gold-record for, 34–36
headquarters move, 101, 136
in Hollywood, 114–15, 121, 124, 136, 137
in-house band, 71–72
international success, 80–81, 99–100
jealousy, drinking in, 100–101
King's speeches by, 77–78, 107, 110, 135
quality-control debates at, 31–32, 34, 35, 38
television shows and, 114–15, 118–19, 120, 134,
    135, 136
Motown Productions, 114, 122, 137
Motown: The Musical, 128, 138
Music City. *See* Detroit
"My Girl," 85, 130, 135
"My Guy," 39–40

Obama, Barack, 128
Off the Wall, 123

Patten, Edward, 89
Payton, Lawrence, *80*, 81–82
"Please Mr. Postman," 41, 49, 80, 134
Powell, Maxine, 56, 83, 95, 98
    as Artist Development head, *54*
    performer etiquette of, 51–53, 59
prejudice, 13, 75
    on Motortown Revue tour, 46–47
    record company, 18
The Primettes. *See* Diana Ross and the Supremes

race music, 2, 14, 91
race riot. *See* Detroit riots
racial crossover, 10, 14, 54, 91, 98, 115
record companies, 80
    touring and, 44
    white ownership of, 18–19
Recorded Live: The 12 Year Old Genius, 69, 80
Recording Industry Association of America, 35
"Reet Petite," 17, 18, 21, 133
Reeves, Martha, 30, 100, *105*. *See also* Martha and the
    Vandellas
Regal Theater, 67
Richie, Lionel, 125, 137
Robertson, Carole, 76, *77*

Robinson, Claudette Rogers, 21, *34*
Robinson, William ("Smokey"), 21, 29, *34*, 35, *36*, 128, 132
    and Gordy, B., *129*, 133
       Hollywood Motown and, 124
       as songwriter, 83–85, 87, 88, 89, 135
Rock and Roll Hall of Fame, 128, 137
Rogers, Bobby, 21, *34*, 83–84
Ross, Diane ("Diana"), *94*, 95, 97, 118, 132
    crossover appeal of, 98, 115
    international success of, *100*
    leaving Motown, 123, 136, 137
    romance with Gordy, B., 121, *122*
Ruffin, David, *83*, 84, *85*, 101

segregation laws, 13, 46, 75
"Shop Around," 34–36, 38, 49, 134
singing pantomime, 57–58, *96*, 97
Smokey Robinson and the Miracles, *34*, 35, *36*. *See also*
       The Miracles
    assassinations song by, 108
    breakup, 124
    Motortown Revue with, 45, 49
Snowden, James K., Jr. ("Scoopy"), 131–32
song distribution, 34
songwriters, 31
    contest, 83–84
    Gordy, B., in, 12, *17*, 18, 19, 133
    Robinson, S., in, 83–85, 87, 88, 89, 135
    teams of, 62–63
The Sound of Motown, 99
Sound of Young America, 2, 92, 107, 129, 132
Standing in the Shadows of Motown, 72
Starr, Edwin, 108, 136
Stevenson, William ("Mickey"), 63, 65
"Stop! In the Name of Love!," *96*, 135
Strong, Barrett, 34, 108, 133, 136
Stubbs, Levi, *80*, 81–82
"Super Freak," 126
The Supremes. *See* Diana Ross and the Supremes

Tarnopol, Nat, 20
Tarplin, Marv, 21

TCB, 114, *115*, 136
television shows, 114–15, 118–19, 120, 134, 135, 136
The Temptations, 82, *83*, 84, 85, 87, 88–89, 92, 123,
      128, 134, 135
    international success of, 99
    racial pride and, 107
    replacing Ruffin, 101
    on *TCB*, 114, *115*, 136
Terry, Mike, *71*
3-D Record Mart, 13, 15, 133
Thriller, 123, *124*
Till, Emmett, *76*, 103
Tillman, Georgeanna, 40
"To Be Loved," 21
touring. *See* Motortown Revue

Veeder, Larry, *71*
Vietnam War, 104–5, 108–12, 137

"War," 108–9, 110, 136
"The Way You Do the Things You Do," 84, 135
Wells, Mary, 60, 68, 134
    early life of, *38*, 39
    as The First Lady of Motown, 40
    Motortown Revue with, 45, 134
    "My Guy" sung by, 39–40
Wesley, Cynthia, 76, *77*
What's Going On, 111–12, 137
"What's Going On," 109, *110*, 111
White, Ronnie, 21, *34*, 65
Whitfield, Norman, *88*, 89–90, 108, 123, 135,
      136
Williams, Otis, 82, *83*, 85, 132
Williams, Paul, 82, *83*
Wilson, Jackie, 11, 17, *18*, 20, 39
Wilson, Mary, *94*, 95, 101
Wonder, Stevie, 70, 80, 92, 128, 134
    "Fingertips" and, 68, *69*, 135
    Martin Luther King Day and, 124, *125*
    Motown beginning of, 65, *66*, 67–68, 134

"You Are Loved," 12